Yet More Wit

Des MacHale

**THIS BOOK IS DEDICATED TO MY GOOD FRIENDS
ANN AND PAUL SLOANE**

Paperback edition first published in Great Britain 1999 by
Prion Books Limited
Imperial Works, Perren Street,
London NW5 3ED

First published in 1998

A catalogue record of this book can be obtained
from the British Library

ISBN 1-85375-337-8

Printed and bound in Great Britain by
Creative Print and Design Wales, Ebbw Vale

Contents

Introduction

This book, together with WIT and MORE WIT, constitutes the world's greatest collection of witty quotes. For this I can claim no credit other than that of collector, editor, distiller and compiler, but I accept full responsibility for my choices. If a quote made me laugh, wince, or say to myself that I really must share this with as many people as possible, then it was included; otherwise it was not. Quite a few of the quotes made me laugh violently and explosively again and again; maybe someday I will collect these very special quotes into a slim volume and make it available only on prescription.

The human race desperately needs laughter, never more so than at the present time, and this has always been true. I humbly submit that the 6,000 witty quotes I have culled from every source imaginable over the past number of years comprise the greatest artistic creation of the human spirit – a creation that I would not swop for any other artistic creation that I know of, be it music, poetry, art or sculpture. They are a cure for depression and despair, and many of the other ailments, physical and psychological, that afflict mankind. My prescription is that the reader take three daily after meals, and they will last a lifetime, because, when finished, they can be started all over again.

I like to think of the many thousands of people who have written or spoken these witty quotes, men and women, alive and dead, as smiling out at us through these pages with a twinkle in their eyes inviting us to partake in their joy, malice, cleverness and wit. Humour and laughter are two of the things that separate us from the animals and are indomitable expressions of human hope and confidence in the future. ENJOY!

Des MacHale
Cork

Art

Art

Painting is the art of protecting flat surfaces from the weather and exposing them to the critic.

Ambrose Bierce

He was the world's only armless sculptor. He used to put the chisel in his mouth and have his wife hit him on the back of the head with a mallet.

Fred Allen

Any fool can paint a picture, but it takes a wise man to be able to sell it.

Samuel Butler

Andy Warhol is the only genius with an IQ of 60.

Gore Vidal

What has happened to architecture since the Second World War that the only passers-by who can contemplate it without pain are those equipped with a white stick and dog?

Bernard Levin

Who among us has not gazed at a painting of Jackson Pollock's and thought 'What a piece of crap'?

Rob Long

Modern art is what happens when painters stop looking at girls and persuade themselves they have a better idea.

John Ciardi

William Orpen never got under the surface until he got under the sod.

Oliver St John Gogarty

A painter who has the feel of breasts and buttocks is saved.

Auguste Renoir

He has returned from Italy a greater bore than ever; he bores on architecture, painting, statuary and music.

Sydney Smith

There are three kinds of people in the world: those who can't stand Picasso, those who can't stand Raphael and those who have never heard of either of them.

John White

Of course William Morris was a wonderful artist and an all-round man, but the art of walking round him has always tired me.

Max Beerbohm

Donner wanted to be an artist because he heard there were opportunities to meet naked women.

Tom Stoppard

A portrait is a painting with something wrong with the mouth.

John S. Sargent

Mona Lisa has the smile of a woman who has just dined off her husband.

Lawrence Durrell

A highbrow is the kind of person who looks at a sausage and thinks of Picasso.

A.P. Herbert

An amateur is an artist who supports himself with outside jobs which enable him to paint. A professional is someone whose wife works to enable him to paint.

Ben Shahn

He will lie even when it is inconvenient, the sign of the true artist.

Gore Vidal

Who is this chap Augustus John? He drinks, he's dirty and I know there are women in the background.

Bernard Montgomery

Turner's *The Slave Ship* resembles a tortoiseshell cat having a fit in a plate of tomatoes.

Mark Twain

Mona Lisa looks as if she has just been sick or is about to be.
Noel Coward

Mr Whistler has always spelled art with a capital 'I'.

Oscar Wilde

If only people knew as much about painting as I do, they would never buy my pictures.

Edwin H. Landseer

Graham Sutherland's portrait of me makes me look as if I were straining at stool.

Winston Churchill

When having my portrait painted I don't want justice, I want mercy.

Billy Hughes

Rembrandt painted 700 pictures. Of these 3000 are in existence.

Wilhelm Bode

If you have a burning restless urge to paint, simply eat something sweet and the feeling will pass.

Fran Lebowitz

An enraged cartoonist burst into the office of the editor of the *New Yorker* and shouted 'You never use my stuff but you publish the work of a fifth rate artist like Thurber.' The editor immediately sprang to my defence. 'Third rate' he said.

James Thurber

Art

The world's worst piece of art is reputed to be *Le Remède* by Antione Watteau. It depicts a reclining Venus about to receive an enema administered by her chambermaid.

Bruce Felton

The day is coming when a single carrot, freshly observed, will set off a revolution.

Paul Cézanne

I'm an artist and in a court of law that's next worst to an actress.

Joyce Cary

The art galleries of Paris contain the finest collection of frames I ever saw.

Humphry Davy

The Acropolis is beige! My colour!

Elsie De Wolfe

Business and Money

Few great men would have got past Personnel.

Paul Goodman

The upper crust is just a bunch of crumbs held together by dough.

Joseph A. Thomas

We don't seem to be able to check crime, so why not legalise it and then tax it out of business?

Will Rogers

The secret of ensuring a man's wealth is when the little beggar is ten years old, have him castrated and his taste buds destroyed. He'll grow up never needing a woman, a steak or a cigarette. Think of the money saved.

W.C. Fields

The only reason I made a commercial for American Express was to pay for my American Express bill.

Peter Ustinov

Every morning I get up and look through the Forbes list of the richest people in America. If I'm not there, I go to work.

Robert Orben

I am proud to be paying taxes in the United States. But I could be just as proud for half the money.

Arthur Godfrey

They were a people so primitive they did not know how to get money except by working for it.

Joseph Addison

Actuaries have the reputation of being about as interesting as the footnotes on a pension plan.

George Pitcher

More and more these days I find myself pondering on how to reconcile my net income with my gross habits.

John Nelson

These are the guidelines for bureaucrats;
1 When in charge, ponder.
2 When in trouble, delegate.
3 When in doubt, mumble.

James H. Boren

Two guys were looking at some shirts in a shop window. One said 'That's the one I'd get', when the owner of the shop, a Cyclops, came out and kicked his head in.

Craig Charles

You can't put your VISA bill on your American Express card.

P.J. O'Rourke

I am very fond of fresh air and royalties.

Daisy Ashford

No real English gentleman, in his secret soul, was ever sorry for the death of a political economist.

Walter Bagehot

What if everything is an illusion and nothing exists. In that case, I definitely overpaid for my carpet.

Woody Allen

To make a million, start with $900,000.

Morton Shulman

A criminal is a person with predatory instincts who has not sufficient capital to form a corporation.

Howard Scott

Money is something you have got to make in case you don't die.

Max Asnas

I came by the racetrack today but it was closed, so I just shoved all my money through the gate.

W.C. Fields

People say sailing is an expensive sport, but to own a racehorse is the equivalent of burning a yacht on the front lawn every year.

Adam Nicholson

I performed badly in the Civil Service examinations because evidently I knew more about economics than my examiners.

J.M. Keynes

Gentlemen prefer bonds.

Andrew Mellon

When you've got them by their wallets, their hearts and minds will follow.

Fern Naito

Most of my contemporaries at school entered the World of Business, the logical destiny of bores.

Barry Humphries

Today you can go to a gas station and find the cash register open and the toilets locked. They must think toilet paper is worth more than money.

Joey Bishop

It is unforgivable to deny racegoers facilities for losing their money swiftly and painlessly.

Hugh McIlvanney

Whoever said money can't buy happiness simply hadn't found out where to go shopping.

Bo Derek

Less than perfect financial circumstances are the keenest spur to further endeavour.

Joe Davis

A bargain is something you can't use at a price you can't resist.

Franklin P. Jones

All I ask is a chance to prove that money can't make me happy.

Spike Milligan

In the business world an executive knows something about everything, a technician knows everything about something – and the switchboard operator knows everything.

Harold Coffin

One is always excited by descriptions of money changing hands. It's much more fundamental than sex.

Nigel Dennis

You walk into an estate agent's office and all the roulette tables become desks.

Dylan Moran

If advertisers spent the same amount of money improving their products as they do on advertising then they wouldn't have to advertise them.

Will Rogers

I handed one of my creditors an IOU and thought thank God that's settled.

Richard Brinsley Sheridan

Never underestimate the effectiveness of a straight cash bribe.

Claud Cockburn

I told the Inland Revenue I didn't owe them a penny because I live near the seaside.

Ken Dodd

It is better to give than to lend, and it costs about the same.

Philip Gibbs

If you think your boss is stupid remember; you wouldn't have a job if he was any smarter.

Albert Grant

Only one fellow in ten thousand understands the currency question, and we meet him every day.

Kin Hubbard

Boswell, lend me sixpence – not to be repaid.

Samuel Johnson

It is better to have a permanent income than to be fascinating.

Oscar Wilde

We didn't actually overspend our budget. The allocation simply fell short of our expenditure.

Keith Davis

It is the height of bad taste to have anything business-related in your briefcase. Briefcases are for taking the contents of the stationery cupboard home with you at the end of the day. Only photocopier repairmen have their work in their briefcases – 15 different screwdrivers, a copy of the Sun and a list of exotic, faraway locations where the vital missing part will have to be supplied from.

Guy Browning

I'm spending a year dead for tax reasons.

Douglas Adams

George Orwell would not blow his nose without moralising on the conditions in the handkerchief industry.

Cyril Connolly

One way to solve the traffic problem would be to keep all the cars that are not paid for off the streets.

Will Rogers

Don't buy shares in companies whose chairmen can play consistently below their handicap. Either they are playing too much golf or they cheat.

Jeff Randall

I am not a paranoid deranged millionaire. Goddamit, I'm a billionaire.

Howard Hughes

There is only one thing for a man to do who is married to a woman who enjoys spending money, and that is to enjoy earning it.

Edgar W. Howe

Consultants are people who borrow your watch to tell you what time it is and then walk off with it.

Robert Townsend

If you owe the bank $100, that's your problem. If you owe the bank $100 million, that's the bank's problem.

John Paul Getty

I have never been in any situation where having money made it worse.

Clinton Jones

The only man who makes money following the horses is one who does it with a broom and shovel.

Elbert Hubbard

Economics is useful only as a form of employment for economists.

J.K. Galbraith

Unquestionably there is progress. The average American now pays out twice as much in taxes as he formerly got in wages.

H.L. Mencken

Anyone who lives within their means suffers from a lack of imagination.

Oscar Wilde

Recession is when your neighbour loses his job. Depression is when you lose yours. And recovery is when Jimmy Carter loses his.

Ronald Reagan

When I come home from the races my wife never asks any questions if I tell her I just ate a $380 hot dog.

Tom Conway

I don't know much about being a millionaire but I'll bet I'd be darling at it.

Dorothy Parker

Ocean racing is like standing under a cold shower tearing up £5 notes.

Edward Heath

When a person with experience meets a person with money, the person with experience will get the money and the person with the money will get some experience.

Leonard Lauder

We don't just honour credit cards – we venerate them!

Dale McFeathers

They say it's better to be poor and happy than rich and miserable. But couldn't some compromise be worked out, like being moderately wealthy and just a little moody?

John Henry

I'd give a thousand dollars to be a millionaire.

Lewis Timberlake

I need enough to tide me over until I need more.

Bill Hoest

What is a thousand dollars? Mere chicken feed. A poultry matter.

Groucho Marx

Part of the $10 million I spent on gambling, part on booze and part on women. The rest I spent foolishly.

George Raft

Drink and other Drugs

Drink and other Drugs

I don't like people who take drugs – like customs men for example.

Mick Miller

It was what I would call a three-man wine – two men had to hold you down so that a third could pour it down your throat.

George Lang

I haven't touched a drop of alcohol since the invention of the funnel.

Malachy McCourt

There is only one thing to be said in favour of drink and that is that it has caused many a lady to be loved that otherwise might have died single.

Peter Finley Dunne

Customers in an Irish pub are asked not to throw lighted cigarette ends on the floor. People leaving have burned their hands and faces.

Tony Butler

Have you heard about the Irishman who joined Alcoholics Anonymous? He still drinks but under a different name.

Aubrey Dillon-Malone

I never drink because I was born intoxicated.

George Russell

I seldom took a drink on the set before 9 a.m.

W.C. Fields

The Bishop was talking to the local Master of Hounds about the difficulty he had in keeping his vicars off the incense.

P.G. Wodehouse

It was a French physician, naturally enough, who first described the disease known as cirrhosis of the liver.

Richard Selzer

The conclusion of your syllogism, I said lightly, is fallacious, being based upon licensed premises.

Flann O'Brien

The best way to cure a hangover is to avoid alcohol the night before.

Cathy Hopkins

I drink too much. Last time I gave a urine sample it had an olive in it.

Rodney Dangerfield

What I like to drink most is wine that belongs to others.

Diogenes

Drink and other Drugs

You suck on that cigarette because you didn't suck on your mom long enough when you were a kid. That's the absolute truth. If I could buy a pack of breasts, I would. I'd be smoking forty to fifty packs a day. I'd be down the news stand first thing every morning: 'Gimme a pack of 44Ds. You can leave the nipples on 'em'.

Denis Leary

Reality is just a crutch for people who cannot cope with drugs.

Robin Williams

The best pitch I ever heard about cocaine was back in the early eighties when a street dealer followed me down the sidewalk going 'I got some great blow man. I got the stuff that killed Belushi'.

Denis Leary

I've stopped drinking. But only while I'm asleep.

George Best

During the war I consumed German wine but I excused myself that I was not drinking it but interning it.

Winston Churchill

I've been told alcohol is a slow poison. I'm in no hurry.

Robert Benchley

Drink and other Drugs

W.C. Fields was fond of playing the golf course sideways with his pal Oliver Hardy. He liked being in the trees where he could drink without scandalising the natives.

Jim Murray

I never drank anything stronger than beer before I was twelve.

W.C. Fields

Prohibition is better than no liquor at all.

Will Rogers

I am so holy that when I touch wine, it turns into water.

Aga Khan III

It was a non-smoker who committed the first sin and brought death into the world and all our woe. Nero was a non-smoker. Lady Macbeth was a non-smoker. Decidedly the record of the non-smokers leaves them little to be proud of.

Robert Lynd

An old wine-bibber having been smashed in a railway collision, some wine was poured on his lips to revive him. 'Pauillac 1873', he murmured and died.

Ambrose Bierce

The Campaign for Real Ale is the last refuge of bearded Trotskyite Morris dancers.

Alun Howkins

Drink and other Drugs

Real ale fans are just like train-spotters, only drunk.
Christopher Howse

There are all sorts of methods of giving up smoking. My aunt used to pour a gallon of petrol over herself every morning. The idea being that she couldn't light up without turning herself into a human fireball. It didn't stop her — she'd be in the living room and you'd hear a cough and a woosh. She was up to forty wooshes a day by the end of it.
Paul Merton

I'm not really a heavy smoker any more. I get through only two lighters a day now.
Bill Hicks

I am a drinker with a writing problem.
Brendan Behan

Spanish wine is foul. Catpiss is champagne compared to this sulphurous urination of some aged horse.
D.H. Lawrence

The worst alcoholic beverage on record was found when two women in Idaho were arrested on charges of manufacturing and selling an ersatz brandy which was distilled from water, vodka and urine.
Mark Fowler

I make it a rule never to smoke while I'm sleeping.
Mark Twain

Drink and other Drugs

Back in my running days, I would tremble and shake for hours upon arising. It was the only exercise I got.

W.C. Fields

The answers to life's problems aren't at the bottom of a bottle, they're on TV.

Homer Simpson

Education

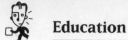

I'm a philosophy major. That means I can think deep thoughts about being unemployed.

Bruce Lee

Smartness runs in my family. When I went to school I was so smart my teacher was in my class for five years.

George Burns

Metaphysics is an attempt to prove the incredible by an appeal to the unintelligible.

H.L. Mencken

What's on your mind, if you will forgive the overstatement?

Fred Allen

Headmasters of schools tend to be men.

Clare Short

He was about to open his lecture, when one of his students rose in his seat and asked a question. It is a practice which, I need hardly say, we do not encourage; the young man, I believe, was a newcomer in the philosophy class.

Stephen Leacock

He respects Owl, because you can't help respecting anybody who can spell TWESDAY, even if he doesn't spell it right.

A.A. Milne

Education

One of my school reports read as follows – 'This boy shows great originality, which must be crushed at all costs'.

Peter Ustinov

A plumber who has Latin is a better plumber than one who does not.

Enoch Powell

I don't think one 'comes down' from Jimmy's university. According to him, it's not even red brick, but white tile.

John Osborne

Hamlet is the tragedy of tackling a family problem too soon after college.

Tom Masson

What did I do for my college? I drank for it.

Evelyn Waugh

I am the Roman Emperor, and am above grammar.

Emperor Sigismund

Macaulay not only overflowed with learning, he stood in the slop.

Sydney Smith

He may be dead; or, he may be teaching English.

Cormac McCarthy

Teenage boys left alone for an evening with an older brother while their parents are out do not study mathematics. They study fratricide.

Mary Riddell

College athletes used to get a degree in bringing your pencil.

Ruby Wax

On many American campuses the only qualification for admission is the ability to find the campus and then discover a parking space.

Malcolm Bradbury

At New York University I majored in advanced fondling. I minored in foreplay.

Woody Allen

The Romans would never have conquered the world if they had to learn Latin first.

Heinrich Heine

The great advantage of an English public school education is that no subsequent form of captivity can hold any particular terror for you. A friend who was put to work on the Burma railway once told me that he was greeted, on arrival, by a fellow prisoner-of-war who said, 'Cheer up. It's not half as bad as Marlborough'.

John Mortimer

Education

Why don't they pass a constitutional amendment prohibiting anybody from learning anything? If it works as good as Prohibition did, in five years Americans would be the smartest race of people on earth.

Will Rogers

I would rather be governed by the first three hundred names in the Boston telephone book than by the Faculty of Harvard University.

William F. Buckley

Grammar schools are public schools without the sodomy.

Tony Parsons

There is nothing as stupid as an educated man, if you get him off the thing he was educated in.

Will Rogers

There is only one thing that consoles me about my exams. They cannot possibly ask everything I don't know.

Stanisfer Ryan

My schooldays were the happiest days of my life – which gives you some idea of the misery I've endured over the past twenty-five years.

Paul Merton

Historians are like deaf people who go on answering questions that no one has asked them.

Leo Tolstoy

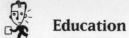

Sixty minutes of thinking of any kind is bound to lead to confusion and unhappiness.

James Thurber

The intellect of the Prince of Wales is of no more use than a pistol packed in the bottom of a trunk in the robber-infested Apennines.

Prince Albert

Your head is as empty as a hermit's address book.

Rowan Atkinson

I was thrown out of NYU for cheating – with the dean's wife.

Woody Allen

My wife was a Latin scholar. On our honeymoon I asked her to conjugate but she declined.

Don Foreman

If I had known I was going to be president of Bolivia, I would have learned to read and write.

Enrique Penaranda

I have been described as 'A lighthouse in the middle of a bog', brilliant but useless.

Conor Cruise O'Brien

Education

Charlemagne either died or was born or did something with the Holy Roman Empire in 800.

Robert Benchley

Chess is the most elaborate waste of human intelligence outside an advertising agency.

Raymond Chandler

An encyclopaedia is a system for collecting dust in alphabetical order.

Mike Barfield

We schoolmasters must temper discretion with deceit.

Evelyn Waugh

Lectures at our university are optional. Graduation is also optional.

Brian Quinn

The founding fathers in their wisdom decided that children were an unnatural strain on parents. So they provided jails called schools, equipped with torture called education.

John Updike

By the time I was thirteen I realised I'd be more successful at something physical rather than mental.

Arnold Schwarzenegger

Food

Food

There are two things in life I like firm and one of them is jelly.

Mae West

A winkle is just a bogey with a crash helmet on.

Mick Miller

I didn't complain about the steak, dear. I merely said I didn't see that old horse that used to be tethered outside here.

W.C. Fields

I was polishing off the last mouthful of a dish in a restaurant when I heard one waiter whisper to another, 'He's actually eating it'.

Gilbert Harding

At big dinners my motto always is 'Eat it now, you can always vomit it later'.

Derek Nimmo

In Spain, attempting to obtain a chicken-salad sandwich, you wind up with a dish whose name, when you look it up in your Spanish-English dictionary, turns out to mean 'Eel with the Big Abscess'.

Dave Barry

I no longer prepared food or drink with more than one ingredient.

Cyra McFadden

The trouble with eating Italian food is that five or six days later you're hungry again.

George Miller

All these cereals they have: Cracklin' Oat Bran and Honkin Fibre Chunks. Cereal used to come with a free prize and now it comes with a roll of toilet paper in every box.

Denis Leary

God invented vegetables to let women get even with their children.

P.J. O'Rourke

For a long time I thought coq au vin meant love in a lorry.

Victoria Wood

Parsley is gharsley.

Ogden Nash

There is no such thing as a little garlic.

Aga Khan III

Whatever you tell them, people always make your tea or coffee the way they like it.

Russell Bell

Ask your child what he wants for dinner only if he's buying.

Fran Lebowitz

There is nothing worse than being stuck up in the Andes Mountains in a plane crash with your anorexic friend Freddy.

Denis Leary

'Escargot' is French for 'fat crawling bag of phlegm'.

Dave Barry

Far too many cooks spoil the broth.

Wayne G. Haisley

Baseball feels better than sex and almost as good as eating watermelon.

Teddy Tannenbaum

The *Mayflower* left Plymouth for Massachusetts to check out some likely sites for MacDonalds restaurants.

Russell Bell

Mexican food is delicious and perfectly safe as long as you are careful never to get any of it in your digestive system.

Dave Barry

Cottage cheese has no flavour – it's like kissing your sister.

Cathy Hopkins

Never serve oysters in a month that has no paycheck in it.

P.J. O'Rourke

Did you ever notice they never take any fat hostages? You never see a guy come out of Lebanon going 'I was held hostage for seven months and I lost 175 pounds. I feel good and I look good and I learned self-discipline. That's the important thing.'

Denis Leary

Turkish food is edible Greek food.

A.A. Gill

I've had matzo ball soup three meals in a row. Isn't there any other part of the matzo you can eat?

Marilyn Monroe

It would be nice if the Food and Drug Administration stopped issuing warnings about toxic substances and just gave me the names of one or two things still safe to eat.

Robert Fuoss

A recipe is a series of step-by-step instructions for preparing ingredients you forgot to buy in utensils you don't own to make a dish the dog won't eat the rest of.

Henry Beard

The food in that restaurant is terrible. And such small portions.

Woody Allen

There are very few shops in the country, but the ever resourceful farm folk have come up with a number of ingenious if disgusting ploys to circumvent this inconvenience. They won't just go out and buy a carton of milk like proper people, so what do they do? They squeeze it out of a cow! God only knows who first came up with that one, but it seems to work. Apparently cows are full of the stuff.

Russell Bell

The chip is the great British contribution to world cuisine.
John Cleese

Organic is just another word for dirty fruit.

Ruby Wax

Easter eggs go on sale for a short period because they are basically horrible. Something happens to chocolate in the process of turning it eggshaped that makes it taste like something that has spent 20 years at the back of a cupboard. The pagan tradition is strong enough to persuade people to pay £3.99 for this experience once a year, but no way are they going to repeat it more often. By the time a year has passed they have forgotten how unpleasant Easter eggs are and they then buy them again.

Robert Crompton

After a good dinner, one can forgive anybody, even one's own relations.

Oscar Wilde

Food

He looked at me as if I was a side dish he hadn't ordered.

Ring Lardner

A good reducing exercise consists of placing both hands against the edge of the table and pushing back.

Robert Quillen

Take those scales out of the bathroom; the right place for them is in front of the refrigerator.

Richard Needham

I work for a company that makes deceptively shallow dishes for Chinese restaurants.

Woody Allen

Extra food is allowed for weddings, golden weddings, funerals and other festivities.

Edith Somerskill M.P.

Anything is good if it's made of chocolate.

Jo Brand

The Texas recipe for chili is to put a pot of chili on the stove to simmer. Let it simmer. Meanwhile, broil a good steak. Eat the steak. Let the chili simmer. Ignore it.

Allan Shivers

Inhabitants of underdeveloped nations and victims of natural disasters are the only people who have ever been happy to see soyabeans.

Fran Lebowitz

Food

The food was so tasteless you could eat a meal of it and belch and it wouldn't remind you of anything.

Red Foxx

My doctor has advised me to give up those intimate little dinners for four, unless there are three people eating with me.

Orson Welles

English vegetables taste as though they have been boiled in a strong soap.

W.C. Fields

I was eating a lot of frozen TV dinners when I realised they would probably taste better if they were warm.

Yakov Smirnoff

I feel the end approaching. Quick, bring me my dessert, coffee, and liqueur.

Pierette Brillat Savarin

Do you know what breakfast cereal is made of? It's made of all those little curly wooden shavings you find in pencil sharpeners.

Roald Dahl

Cantonese will eat anything in the sky but airplanes, anything in the sea but submarines and anything with four legs but the table.

Amanda Bennett

Bertrand Russell looked like a vegetarian vulture.

A.A. Gill

Most vegetarians I ever see looked enough like their food to be classed as cannibals.

Finley Peter Dunne

Who bothers to cook TV dinners! I suck them frozen.

Woody Allen

One of the most popular Soviet meals is the bread sandwich. That is two slices of bread with another slice of bread in between. They have the same thing in America – it's called a Big Mac.

Yakov Smirnoff

The most dangerous food is wedding cake.

James Thurber

On ringing a restaurant to ask if they had wheelchair access I was told that they accepted all major credit cards.

Pat Fitzpatrick

The perfect lover is one who turns into a pizza at 4 a.m.

Charles Pierce

When compelled to cook, I produce a meal that would make a sword swallower gag.

Russell Baker

I believe that if I ever had to practise cannibalism, I might manage if there was enough tarragon around.

James Beard

Every morning I get up and I make instant coffee and I drink it so I'll have enough energy to make regular coffee.

Steven Wright

The dumbing-down of notices on food packets has just about reached its limit. I recently bought a packet of peanuts and it said CONTAINS: PEANUTS. INSTRUCTIONS: OPEN PACKET, EAT CONTENTS.

Robin Young

Why is a carrot more orange than an orange?

Ambrose Dukes

I eat like a vulture: unfortunately, the resemblance doesn't end there.

Groucho Marx

My Uncle Joe was a philosopher, very deep, very serious. Never eat chocolate after chicken he'd tell us, wagging his finger.

Mel Brooks

The first time I fried organic wheat bread, I thought I was chewing on roofing material.

Robin Williams

Gélée of duck has the consistency of Pamela Anderson Lee's implants, and was so salty and horrid it was like licking an Abyssinian shotputter's armpit.

A.A. Gill

Age does not diminish the extreme disappointment of having a scoop of ice cream fall from the cone.

Jim Fiebig

Avoid beans as you would matricide.

Pythagoras

Dining on durian is like eating vanilla custard in a latrine.

Anthony Burgess

A nutrient is a chemical added to breakfast cereal to allow it to be sold as a food.

Mike Barfield

Vegetarians have wicked, shifty eyes and laugh in a cold, calculating manner. They pinch little children, steal stamps, drink water and grow beards.

J.B. Morton

I don't eat fish. They are my friends.

Johnny Weissmuller

Food

Women should try to increase their size rather than decrease it, because I believe the bigger we are, the more space we'll take up, and the more we'll have to be reckoned with.

Roseanne Barr

Edible adj: good to eat, and wholesome to digest, as a worm to a toad, a toad to a snake, a snake to a pig, a pig to a man, and a man to a worm.

Ambrose Bierce

This piece of cod passes all understanding.

Edwin Lutyens

By the time they had diminished from 50 to 8, the other dwarfs began to suspect 'Hungry'.

Gary Larson

I've known what it is to be hungry, but I always went right to a restaurant.

Ring Lardner

I personally prefer a nice frozen TV dinner at home, mainly because it's so little trouble. All you have to do is have another drink while you're throwing it in the garbage.

Jack Douglas

The reason there is such a food shortage in Russia is that the government stockpiles all the food for the army. Whatever the army doesn't use after a year, the government sells to the public.

Yakov Smirnoff

Processed 'cheese'. The word should always, like Soviet 'democracy' be framed in quotes, for no matter what the law may say, I refuse to call this cheese. The best I can say for it is that it is not poisonous. The worst, that it represents the triumph of technology over conscience. In the preparation of this solidified floor wax, every problem is solved: packaging, keeping, distribution, slicing, cost. One problem alone is not solved: that of making cheese.

Bob Brown

Lawyers and other Professions

Lawyers and other Professions

My friend Malcolm is a very shy and sensitive used car salesman.

Benny Hill

I remember once going into an undertakers, lying on the floor, and shouting 'shop'.

Spike Milligan

I have knowingly defended a number of guilty men, but the guilty never escape unscathed. My fees are sufficient punishment for anyone.

F. Lee Bailey

A popular Washington stop is the Supreme Court, where the justices frequently ask the spectators to help them decide a tough case by registering their opinions on the applause-o-meter.

Dave Barry

The O.J. Simpson jury they ended up choosing had to swear they'd never heard about a case that had been in the papers every day for a year and a half. And then they ask them to rule on DNA. These idiots didn't even get that far in the alphabet. They wondered why the N came before the A.

Jackie Mason

To escape jury duty in England, wear a bowler hat and carry a rolled-up copy of the *Daily Telegraph*.

John Mortimer

Lawyers and other Professions

The Metropolitan Police Force is abbreviated to the MET to give more members a chance of spelling it.

Mike Barfield

Reading isn't an occupation we encourage among police officers. We try to keep the paperwork down to a minimum.

Joe Orton

Fear of the policeman is the beginning of wisdom.

Charles Pasqua

Even if a farmer intends to loaf, he gets up in time to get an early start.

Edgar W. Howe

If brains were a virus, policemen would be the healthiest people in the world.

John O'Dwyer

In England, justice is open to all – like the Ritz Hotel.

James Mathew

The one great principle of the English law is to make business for itself.

Charles Dickens

Detectives are just policemen with smaller feet.

Whitfield Crook

Make crime pay – become a lawyer.

Will Rogers

Lawyers and other Professions

There are four kinds of homicide: felonious, excusable, justifiable and praiseworthy.

Ambrose Bierce

The physician can bury his mistakes but the architect can only advise his client to plant vines.

Frank Lloyd Wright

Can't wait to be arrested and go all the way to the witness stand. 'Do you swear to tell the whole truth and nothing but the truth, so help you God?' 'Yes. You're ugly. See that woman in the jury? I really fancy her. Should I keep going or are you going to ask me questions?'

Steven Wright

I thought I was an honest guy, and just doing what everyone else was doing – bending the rules.

Manny Goldstein

The Russian police have a Missing Persons Department; that's where they decide which persons are going to be missing.

Yakov Smirnoff

I was ashamed of being a lawyer, so now I manually masturbate caged animals for artificial insemination.

Virginia Smith

A man was beaten up and robbed and lay dying on the roadside. A social worker came along and said, 'Tell me the name of the man who did this. He needs help immediately.'

Murray Watts

Lawyers and other Professions

A man may as well open an oyster without a knife, as a lawyer's mouth without a fee.

Barten Holyday

I would much prefer to be a judge rather than a coal miner because of the absence of falling coal.

Peter Cook

The only way you can beat the lawyers is to die with nothing.

Will Rogers

The finding of a gibbet in an unexplored part of Africa gave me infinite pleasure as it proved that I was in a civilised society.

Mungo Park

Injustice is relatively easy to bear; what stings is justice.

H.L. Mencken

Mr Haughey cannot be named for legal reasons.

Charlie Crow

The only difference between a dead skunk lying on the road and a dead lawyer lying on the road is that there are skid marks near the skunk.

Patrick Murray

Most journalists of my generation died early, succumbing to one or other of the two great killers in the craft – cirrhosis or terminal alimony.

John Hepworth

The function of the expert is not to be more right than other people but to be wrong for more sophisticated reasons.

David Butler

A crowded police court docket is the surest of all signs that trade is brisk and money plenty.

Mark Twain

The only difference between a female lawyer and a pit bull terrier is the lipstick.

Patrick Murray

My will is as follows: count up the lawyers in the state and divide my money among them. If there should by any miracle be any left, let my relatives all of them, God bless 'em, fight over it.

Will Rogers

A group of white South Africans recently killed a black laywer because he was black. That was wrong. They should have killed him because he was a lawyer.

Whitney Brown

Happiness is your dentist telling you it won't hurt and then having him catch his hand on the drill.

Johnny Carson

Lawyers and other Professions

A lawyer with his briefcase can steal more than a thousand men with guns.

Mario Puzo

A lot of people criticise supermodels and I think that's very unfair, because they can't answer back.

Jo Brand

A leading authority is anyone who has guessed right more than once.

Frank Clark

Some tortures are physical and some are mental, but the one that's both is dental.

Ogden Nash

Literature

Fiction writing is great. You can make up almost anything.

Ivana Trump

It's not a good idea to put your wife into a novel – not your latest wife anyway.

Norman Mailer

If you are in difficulties with a book, try the element of surprise; attack it at an hour when it isn't expecting it.

H.G. Wells

I was reading Proust for the first time. Very poor stuff. I think he was mentally defective.

Evelyn Waugh

Kingsley Amis once said that sex is a great cure for a hangover, which, indeed must be the case, because if you thought Kingsley Amis was going to make love to you, you'd certainly avoid getting drunk in the first place.

Joseph O'Connor

Blurbs that appear on the back cover are written by friends of the author who haven't read the book but owe the poor guy a favour.

Art Buchwald

The principle of procrastinated rape is said to be the ruling one in all the great best-sellers.

V.S. Pritchett

Literature

One of the greatest creations of the human mind is the art of reviewing books without having to read them.

G.C. Lichtenberg

Vita Sackville-West looked like Lady Chatterley above the waist and the gamekeeper below.

Cyril Connolly

Dorothy Thompson is the only woman who had her menopause in public and got paid for it.

Alice Roosevelt

I like to take a Trollope to bed, but if one is not available, I will settle for a Wodehouse.

Harold MacMillan

Last time I was in Spain I got through six Jeffrey Archer novels. I must remember to bring enough toilet paper next time.

Bob Monkhouse

I hope you get as much pleasure reading my book as I got spending the money you paid me for it.

Dan Poynter

Anthologies are just pre-digested food for the brain.

Rebecca West

In Australia, not reading poetry is the national pastime.

Phyllis McGinley

Literature

Evelyn Waugh's style has the desperate jauntiness of an orchestra fiddling away for dear life on a sinking ship.

Edmund Wilson

I can write better than anyone who can write faster, and I can write faster than anyone who can write better.

A.J. Liebling

Victor Hugo was a madman who thought he was Victor Hugo.

Jean Cocteau

I should like to see a custom introduced of readers who are pleased with a book sending the author some small cash token: anything between half-a-crown and a hundred pounds. Not more than a hundred pounds – that would be bad for my character – not less than half-a-crown – that would do no good to yours.

Cyril Connolly

The Sitwells belong to the history of publicity rather than of poetry.

F.R. Leavis

The high-water mark so to speak, of Socialist literature is W.H. Auden, a sort of gutless Kipling.

George Orwell

Literature

If we wish to know the force of human genius, we should read Shakespeare. If we wish to see the insignificance of human learning, we may study his commentators.

William Hazlitt

Word has somehow got around that the split infinitive is always wrong. That is of a piece with the outworn notion that it is always wrong to strike a lady.

James Thurber

Outside of a dog, a book is a man's best friend and inside a dog it's too dark to read.

Groucho Marx

How come there's no other name for thesaurus?

Wright Stevens

I always start writing with a clean piece of paper and a dirty mind.

Patrick Dennis

The only reason I visit my friends is so I can look over my own library.

Walter Scott

If even all my ex-girlfriends buy my book it will be a best-seller.

Rod Hundley

I will not meet Swinburne because I have no wish to know anyone sitting in a sewer and adding to it.

Thomas Carlyle

I make it a policy not to read reviews. Instead, I measure them with a ruler. The longer they are the better I feel.

Joseph Conrad

I read half of my autobiography, then I skipped through. I know what it's about though.

Dominique Morceau

Book reviewers are little old ladies of both sexes.

John O'Hara

Agatha Christie has given more pleasure in bed than any other woman.

Nancy Banks-Smith

Isn't it a shame that Maxwell Anderson's poetic licence has expired.

Noel Coward

The most important thing for poets to do is to write as little as possible.

T.S. Eliot

I adore adverbs; they are the only qualifications I really much respect.

Henry James

I have no sense of humour. In illustration of this fact I will say this – by way of confession – that if there is a humorous passage in the *Pickwick Papers* I have never been able to find it.

Mark Twain

Write something, even if it's just a suicide note.

Gore Vidal

One of the surest signs of Conrad's genius is that women dislike his works.

George Orwell

Gertrude Stein and me are just like brothers.

Ernest Hemingway

In cases of any impudent literary letters from married women, I write to the husband warning him that his wife is attempting to enter into correspondence with strange men.

Evelyn Waugh

One watches Stephen Spender use the English language with the same horrified fascination as watching a Sèvres vase in the hands of a chimpanzee.

Evelyn Waugh

Curll's inaccurate biographies are one of the new terrors of death.

John Arbuthnot

Beware of the man who denounces women writers – his penis is tiny and he cannot spell.

Erica Jong

H.G. Wells throws information at the reader as if emptying his mind like a perpetual chamber pot from a window.

Henry James

Mr Wordsworth never ruined anyone's morals, unless, perhaps, he has driven some susceptible persons to crime in a very fury of boredom.

Ezra Pound

The writings of Henry Brougham are long and vigorous, like the penis of a jackass.

Sydney Smith

If you imagine a Scotch commercial traveller in a Scotch commercial hotel leaning on the bar and calling the barmaid Dearie, then you will know the keynote of Burns' verse.

A.E. Housman

Joseph Heller's *God Knows* even looks exactly like a real book, with pages and print and dust jacket and everything. This disguise is extremely clever, considering the contents; the longest lounge act never performed in the history of the Catskills.

Paul Gray

Literature

The book I would most like to have with me on a desert island is *Thomas's Guide to Practical Shipbuilding*.

G.K. Chesterton

I am always glad when one of those poets dies for then I know I have all of his works on my shelf.

George Crabbe

Honest criticism is hard to take particularly from a relative, a friend, an acquaintance or a stranger.

Franklin P. Jones

What would I do if I had only had six months to live? I'd type faster.

Isaac Asimov

The difference between reality and fiction is that fiction has to make sense.

Tom Clancy

The main difference nowadays between poetry and prose is that, dreadful though it is, poetry doesn't go on for nearly so long.

Richard Ingrams

Poets are often described as dealing with the big wide world in a 'childlike' way. Presumably this means that they are always knocking things over, tearing things up and screaming blue murder if they don't get their own way.

Craig Brown

Literature

There is nothing as rare as a Woollcott first edition except perhaps a Woollcott second edition.

Franklin P. Adams

Writing a poem is a bit like being sick. It is quick and efficient and you always feel better afterwards.

Sara-Jane Lovett

The only imaginative fiction being written today is income tax returns.

Herman Wouk

I wrote a few children's books – not on purpose.

Derek Alder

I've sold too many books to get good reviews any more.

John Grisham

Living — Family and Relations

There are few things more satisfying than seeing your children have teenagers of their own.

Doug Larson

Human beings are the only creatures on earth that allow their children to come back home.

Bill Cosby

One thing they never tell you about child-raising is that for the rest of your life, at the drop of a hat, you are expected to know your child's name and how old he or she is.

Erma Bombeck

All the men in my family were bearded, and most of the women.

W.C. Fields

I never want to become pregnant, ever. To me life is tough enough without having someone kick you from the inside.

Rita Rudner

I never saw my grandad because he was excellent at hiding.

Harry Hill

As a housewife, I feel that if the kids are still alive when my husband gets home from work, then hey, I've done my job.

Roseanne Barr

My teenage son is half-man, half mattress.

Val Valentine

My parents used to beat the shit out of me. And, looking back on it I'm glad they did. And I'm looking forward to beating the shit out of my own kids. For no reason whatsoever.

Denis Leary

The only thing I've ever been able to figure out about stove cleaning is to move house every couple of years.

P.J. O'Rourke

You're really old when your family talk about you in front of you. Where are we going to put Pop? We've got company coming over.

Rodney Dangerfield

When Mrs Thatcher said, 'We are a grandmother,' she was including Denis in her remarks.

James Prior

I slept like a baby. Every three hours I woke up looking for a bottle.

Liam O'Reilly

When you are eight years old, nothing is any of your business.

Lenny Bruce

I have a stepladder. It's a very nice stepladder but it's sad that I never knew my real ladder.

Craig Charles

An empty fridge is something you come to expect when you live through the locust phase of adolescence.

Ellen Goodman

My father had a philosophy in life. He used to say 'I brought you into being and if you do that again I'll take you out of it.'

Adrian Walsh

Tired mothers find that spanking takes less time than reasoning and penetrates sooner to the seat of memory.

Will Durant

I phoned my dad to tell him I had stopped smoking. He called me a quitter.

Steven Pearl

Of all my wife's relations I like myself the best.

Joe Cook

In spite of the cost of living, it's still popular.

Kathleen Norris

Living — Family and Relations

I think the delivery room should have traffic noise and pollution. The baby should then have the option to go back in.

Rita Rudner

To lose one parent, Mr Worthing, may be regarded as a misfortune; to lose both looks like carelessness.

Oscar Wilde

My idea of fatherhood is sending a telegram from Abyssinia saying 'Have you had your child yet, and what have you called it?'

Evelyn Waugh

My dad was a kind of father figure to me.

Alan Coren

For toddlers I suggest leaving their mittens on year-round, indoors and out. That way they can't get into aspirin bottles, liquor cabinets or boxes of kitchen matches. Also, it keeps their little hands clean for mealtimes.

P.J. O'Rourke

Never underestimate a child's ability to get into more trouble.

Martin Mull

Don't bother discussing sex with small children. They rarely have anything to add.

Fran Lebowitz

You may go into the fields or down the lane, but don't go into Mr McGregor's garden: your father had an accident there; he was put in a pie by Mrs McGregor.

Beatrix Potter

I advise you to go on living solely to enrage those who are paying your annuities. It is the only pleasure I have left.

Voltaire

It's hard to lose a mother-in-law. In fact it's almost impossible.

W.C. Fields

My eleven-year-old daughter mopes around the house all day waiting for her breasts to grow.

Bill Cosby

We had bad luck with our kids – they all grew up.

Christopher Morley

If this is dying, then I don't think much of it.

Lytton Strachey

The trouble with incest is that it gets you involved with relatives.

George S. Kaufman

I sometimes wish my father realised he was poor instead of being that most nerve-racking of phenomena, a rich man without money.

Peter Ustinov

Don't tell your kids you had an easy birth or they won't respect you. For years I used to wake my daughter up and say 'Melissa you ripped me to shreds. Now go back to sleep.'

Joan Rivers

If you're killed, you've lost a very important part of your life.

Brooke Shields

The man who owns his own house is always just coming out of a hardware store.

Kin Hubbard

When I was a teenager, every Saturday night I'd ask my father for the car keys and he'd always say the same thing: 'All right, son, but don't lose them, because some day we may get a car'.

Yakov Smirnoff

My fiancé's father said to me, 'If you're going to be my son-in-law, you needn't go on calling me "Sir"… Call me "Field Marshal"'.

John Betjeman

John Crowne did have some genius but Crowne's mother and my father were very well acquainted.

John Dryden

They tell you that you'll lose your mind when you grow older. What they don't tell you is that you won't miss it very much.

Malcolm Crowley

I don't want to achieve immortality through my work – I want to achieve it through not dying.

Woody Allen

When Fortune empties her chamberpot on your head, smile and say, 'We are going to have a summer shower.'

John A. MacDonald

Housework is what a woman does that nobody notices unless she hasn't done it.

Evan Esar

When guests stay too long, try treating them like the rest of the family. If they don't leave then, they never will.

Martin Ragaway

Mom and Pop were just a couple of kids when they got married. He was 18, she was 16 and I was 3.

Billie Holiday

You know when you put a stick in the water and it looks like it's bent but it really isn't? That's why I don't take baths.

Steven Wright

When you have told anyone you have left him a legacy, the only decent thing to do is to die at once.

Samuel Butler

Living — Family and Relations

Blood is thicker than water and much more difficult to get out of the carpet.

Woody Allen

You're getting old when the girl you smile at thinks you're one of her father's friends.

Arthur Murray

We must believe in luck, for how else can we explain the success of those we don't like?

Jean Cocteau

I believe in large families; every one should have at least three husbands.

Zsa Zsa Gabor

I smoke ten to fifteen cigars a day — at my age I have to hold on to something.

George Burns

Our family was so poor we used to go to Kentucky Fried Chicken and lick other people's fingers.

Lenny Banks

My unhealthy affection for my second daughter has waned. I now despise all of my seven children equally.

Evelyn Waugh

Have you ever been in therapy? No? You should try it. It's like a really easy game show where the correct answer to every question is: 'Because of my mother'.

Robin Greenspan

No wonder people are so horrible when they start life as children.

Kingsley Amis

They were a tense and peculiar family, the Oedipuses, weren't they?

Max Beerbohm

It was one of those weddings where the bride's and groom's families stood out like opposing football teams, wearing their colours. All the decent hats were, thank God, on our side.

Barbara Trapido

Be kind to your mother-in-law, and if necessary, pay for her board at some good hotel.

Josh Billings

My mother-in-law is so fat, she has her own ZIP code.

Phyllis Diller

The only sense I can make out of having kids is that it's a good way to become a grandparent.

Ralph Noble

Try flying any plane with a baby if you want a sense of what it must have been like to be a leper in the fourteenth century.

Nora Ephron

I don't want to adopt. Not with my genes. I have award-winning genes.

Woody Allen

The Grand Canyon – what a marvellous place to drop one's mother-in-law.

Ferdinand Foch

I decided to have a vasectomy after a family vote on the matter. The kids voted for it eleven to three.

Bob Fraser

One Christmas things were so bad in our house that I asked Santa Claus for a yo-yo and all I got was a piece of string. My father told me it was a yo.

Brendan O'Carroll

The awe and dread with which the untutored savage contemplates his mother-in-law are amongst the most familiar facts of anthropology.

J. G. Frazer

Yes I did take money from children's piggy banks, but I always left my IOU.

W.C. Fields

It's not that I'm afraid to die. I just don't want to be there when it happens.

Woody Allen

No matter how old a mother is, she watches her middle-aged children for signs of improvement.

Florida Scott-Maxwell

I am not the head of our household – but I am the chairman of the fund-raising committee.

Don Foreman

The world is filled with willing people; some willing to work, the rest willing to let them.

Robert Frost

Induction of labour is an obstetric procedure which has brought considerable benefit to man as it reduces the number of duty staff required at week-ends and public holidays.

Don Foreman

Two can live as cheaply as one for half as long.

Howard Kandel

A Freudian slip is when you say one thing when you're really thinking about a mother.

Cliff Claven

Most human problems can be solved by an appropriate charge of high explosive.

Blaster Bates

I once bought my kids a set of batteries for Christmas with a note attached saying TOYS NOT INCLUDED.

Bernard Manning

The trouble with unemployment is that the minute you wake up in the morning, you're on the job.

Lena Horne

Even very young children need to be informed about dying. Explain the concept of death very carefully to your child. This will make threatening him with it much more effective.

P.J. O'Rourke

An optimist is just a guy who has never had much experience.

Don Marquis

I don't like work even when someone else does it.

Mark Twain

Laziness is nothing more than the habit of resting before you get tired.

Jules Renard

Dust is a protective coating for fine furniture.

Mario Buatha

Living — Family and Relations

Everyone seems to fear dying alone and I have never understood this point of view. Who wants to have to die and be polite at the same time?

Quentin Crisp

I don't have anything against work. I just figure, why deprive somebody who really enjoys it?

Dobie Gillis

You've got the brain of a four-year-old boy, and I bet he was glad to get rid of it.

Groucho Marx

Our terraced house was so small the mice walked about on their back legs.

Les Dawson

The longer I live the more I see that I am never wrong about anything and that all the pains I have so humbly taken to verify my notions have only wasted my time.

George Bernard Shaw

Why do we have to die? As a kid you get nice litle white shoes with white laces and a velvet suit with short pants and a nice collar and you go to college, you meet a nice girl and get married, work a few years and then you have to die! What is this shit? They never wrote that in the contract.

Mel Brooks

This year one third of the nation will be ill-nourished, ill-housed, and ill-clad. Only they call it summer vacation.

Joseph Salak

Observing the ancient housekeeper wrestling with the plantlife in the garden, I occasionally point out a weed and encourage her from the deckchair.

Arthur Marshall

Happiness is sitting down to watch some slides of your neighbour's vacation and finding out he spent two weeks in a nudist colony.

Johnny Carson

Parents are not interested in justice, they are interested in peace and quiet.

Bill Cosby

Any fool can criticise, condemn, and complain, and most of them do.

Dale Carnegie

The great comfort of turning forty-nine is the realisation that you are now too old to die young.

Paul Dickson

Heredity is what sets the parents of a teenager wondering about each other.

Laurence J. Peter

Lactomangulation is the act of manhandling the 'open here' spout on a milk carton so badly that one has to resort to using the 'illegal' side.

Rich Hall

Babies don't need a vacation but I still see them at the beach.
I'll go over to a little baby and say, 'What are you doing here?
You've never worked a day in your life.'

Steven Wright

Madam, there's no such thing as a tough child – if you boil
them first for a few hours, they always come out tender.

W.C. Fields

The worst eternal triangle known is teenager, parent and
telephone.

Lavonne Mathison

Love, Sex, Marriage, Men and Women

Women; can't live with them, can't bury them in the back yard without the neighbours seeing.

Sean Williamson

When authorities warn you of the dangers of sex, there is an important lesson to be learned. Do not have sex with the authorities.

Matt Groening

Men should be like Kleenex – soft, strong and disposable.

Cher

The three words you don't want to hear, while making love are 'Honey I'm home'.

Ken Hammond

An eighty-year-old friend of mine has just returned from his honeymoon with his eighteen-year-old bride. He described it as like trying to force a marshmallow into a piggy bank.

Keith Waterhouse

Everyone should be married. A bachelor's life is no life for a single man.

Sam Goldwyn

The time you spend grieving over a man should never exceed the amount of time you actually spent with him.

Rita Rudner

Don't have sex man. It leads to kissing and pretty soon you've got to talk to them.

Steve Martin

Women complain about premenstrual syndrome, but I think of it as the only time of the month I can be myself.

Roseanne Barr

Like most men, I am consumed with desire whenever a lesbian gets within 20 feet.

Taki

She was so sweet that we just walked in the park and I was so touched by her that after fifteen minutes I wanted to marry her and, after half an hour, I completely gave up the idea of snatching her purse.

Woody Allen

If a woman insists on being called Ms ask her if that stands for miserable.

Russell Bell

Give a man a free hand and he'll run it all over you.

Mae West

You should always be missing some buttons. It's part of your boyish bachelor charm. Many a woman has sat down on the living-room couch to sew a button and has wound up doing something more interesting on another piece of furniture elsewhere in the room.

P.J. O'Rourke

Women asserted that they would not be dictated to but then went out and became stenographers.

G.K. Chesterton

I don't know the question, but sex is definitely the answer.

Woody Allen

They were not so much her private parts as her public parts.

Alan Bennett

Golf and sex are the only things you can enjoy without being any good at them.

Jimmy Demaret

There was not much wrong with Virginia Woolf except that she was a woman.

Germaine Greer

During my army medical, they asked me if I was homosexual. I said I wasn't but I was willing to learn.

Bill Murray

When I eventually met Mr Right, I had no idea his first name was 'Always'.

Rita Rudner

Under twenty-one women are protected by law; over sixty-five they're protected by nature; anything in between is fair game.

Cary Grant

There is at least one fool in every married couple.

Henry Fielding

Women are nothing but machines for producing children.

Napoleon Bonaparte

Sex is one of the most wholesome, beautiful and natural things that money can buy.

Steve Martin

When thou goest to woman, take thy whip.

Friedrich Nietzsche

You have to go back to the Children's Crusade in AD 1212 to find as unfortunate and fatuous attempt at manipulated hysteria as the Women's Liberation Movement.

Helen Lawrenson

I was asked if I would support the 18 compromise in the coming debate on the age of homosexual consent in the House of Lords, but I must have been reading the bill upside down because I thought it said 81, which did seem most unfair.

William Temple

The others were only my wives. But you my dear, my fifth wife, will also be my widow.

Sacha Guitry

I had the upbringing a nun would envy. Until I was fifteen I was more familiar with Africa than my own body.

Joe Orton

My wife's hands are so beautiful that I'm going to have a bust made of them.

Sam Goldwyn

Any married man should forget his mistakes – no use two people remembering the same thing.

Duane Dewel

A married couple are well suited when both partners usually feel the need for a quarrel at the same time.

Jean Rostand

A man should be taller, older, heavier, uglier and hoarser than his wife.

Edgar W. Howe

If you cannot have your dear husband for a comfort and a delight, for a crosspatch, for a sofa, chair or a hotwater bottle, one can use him as a Cross to be Borne.

Stevie Smith

She is a peacock in everything but beauty.

Oscar Wilde

Another reason girls talk earlier than boys is breastfeeding. Boys would rather breastfeed than talk because they know they won't be getting that close again for another fifteen years.

Paul Seaburn

I wouldn't be caught dead marrying a woman old enough to be my wife.

Tony Curtis

You're getting old if you discuss the facts of life with your children and you get slapped by your wife when you attempt to try out some of the things they told you.

Russell Bell

Men have simple needs. They can survive the whole weekend with only three things: beer, boxer shorts, and batteries for the remote control.

Diana Jordan

When I was your age, I had been an inconsolable widower for three months, and was already paying my addresses to your admirable mother.

Oscar Wilde

Ask a toad what is beauty? A female with two great round eyes coming out of her little head, a large flat mouth, a yellow belly and a brown back.

Voltaire

A woman voting for divorce is like a turkey voting for Christmas.

Alice Glynn

Before we make love, my husband takes a painkiller.

Joan Rivers

If you want a good sex life the answer is communication. If you're making love to your partner, tell her.

Ivor Dembina

I have no boobs whatsoever. On my wedding night my husband said, 'Let me help you with those buttons' and I told him, 'I'm completely naked'.

Joan Rivers

Hanging on to a bad relationship is like chewing gum after the flavour is gone.

Rita Rudner

I have never married because I cannot mate in captivity.

Gloria Steinem

Conventional intercourse is like squeezing jam into a doughnut.

Germaine Greer

Breathes there a man with hide so tough,
Who says two sexes aren't enough?

Samuel Hoffenstein

Love, Sex, Marriage...

Men carry their brains lower than women do, so when their scratching their crotches, they're not being gross – they're just thinking.

Diana Jordan

The best way to remember your wife's birthday is to forget it once.

Joseph Cossman

Even the most respectable woman has a complete set of clothes in her wardrobe ready for a possible abduction.

Sacha Guitry

I would rather see a woman die, any day, than see her happy with someone else.

Pablo Picasso

There comes a moment in the day, when you have written your pages in the morning, attended to your correspondence in the afternoon, and have nothing further to do. Then comes the hour when you are bored; that's the time for sex.

H.G. Wells

After we made love he took a piece of chalk and made an outline of my body.

Joan Rivers

I'm all for women's rights – and for their lefts too.

Groucho Marx

To please my wife, I decided to get in touch with my feminine side. Now I've got a yeast infection.

Bob Delaney

You can tell how long a couple has been married by whether they are on their first, second or third bottle of Tabasco sauce.

Bruce R. Bye

Men aren't attracted to me by my mind. They are attracted to me by what I don't mind.

Gypsy Rose Lee

A sexagenarian, at his age, I think that's disgusting.

Gracie Allen

I save a fortune on plastic surgery. I just always turn the lights out.

Phyllis Diller

The secret of a successful marriage is not to be at home too much.

Colin Chapman

We have a saying in Russia, 'Women are like buses'. That's it.

Yakov Smirnoff

My girlfriend said to me in bed the other night, 'You're a pervert'. I said to her 'That's a big word for a girl of nine'.

Emo Philip

When I was told that by the year 2100 women would rule the world, I replied 'Still?'

Winston Churchill

In my house I'm the boss. My wife is just the decision maker.

Woody Allen

It was partially my fault that we got divorced. I tended to put my wife under a pedestal.

Woody Allen

Conrad Hilton gave me a very generous divorce settlement. I wound up with 5000 Gideon Bibles.

Zsa Zsa Gabor

The essential difference between men and women is that if you ask a woman how she feels, sooner or later you'll hear about every relationship she's ever been in. Ask a man what he feels and he'll tell you he feels like a pizza.

Diana Ford

Is sex dirty? Only if it's done right.

Woody Allen

Don't knock masturbation – it's sex with someone you love.

Woody Allen

Marrying for love is a very recent idea. In the old country, they didn't marry for love. A man married a woman because he needed an extra mule.

Woody Allen

The appropriate age for marriage is about eighteen for girls and thirty-seven for men.

Aristotle

A wise woman will always let her husband have her way.

Richard Brinsley Sheridan

I once read about a species of fish wherein the male is much smaller than the female, and when he mates with her, he becomes permanently stuck to her, and she sort of absorbs him until he is actually part of her body, just an appendage of the female, kind of like whoever is currently married to Elizabeth Taylor.

Dave Barry

I've finally figured out that being male is the same thing more or less, as having a personality disorder.

Carol Shields

If thee marries for money, thee surely will earn it.

Ezra Bowen

Marriage is the most advanced form of warfare in the modern world.

Malcolm Bradbury

I asked her if she was doing anything on Saturday night and she told me she was committing suicide. So I asked her if she was doing anything on Friday night.

Woody Allen

I had a love-hate relationship with one of my husbands. He loved me, I hated him.

Zsa Zsa Gabor

Have I ever paid for sex? Only emotionally.

Lee Hurst

James Hunt used to write me love letters from all over the world. Well, not actually love letters. They were more like technical reports on his car.

Taormina Rich

Beware of the man who picks your dresses; he wants to wear them.

Erica Jong

A man and wife should never have it in their power to hang one another.

George Farquhar

I don't know if my first experience was heterosexual or homosexual because I was too polite to ask.

Gore Vidal

A lady, if surprised by melancholy, might go to bed with a chap, once; or a thousand times if consumed by passion. But twice my dear fellow, twice, a lady might think she'd been taken for a tart.

Tom Stoppard

Love, Sex ,Marriage...

My wife doesn't care what I do when I'm away as long as I don't have a good time.

Lee Trevino

Marriage is a matter of give and take. You better give it to her, or she'll take it anyway.

Joey Adams

My wife got the house, the car, the bank account, and if I marry again and have children, she gets them too.

Woody Allen

'Tis safest in matrimony to begin with a little aversion.

Richard Brinsley Sheridan

Have you ever started dating someone because you were too lazy to commit suicide?

Judy Tenuta

I gave my beauty and youth to men. I am going to give my wisdom and experience to animals.

Brigitte Bardot

Women run everything. The only thing I have decided in my house over the last twenty years is to recognise Angola as an independent state.

Brian Clough

I believe it is possible to obtain a divorce in the United States on the grounds of incompatibility. If that is true, I am surprised there are any marriages left in the United States.

G.K. Chesterton

Joan Collins unfortunately can't be with us tonight. She's busy attending the birth of her next husband.

John Parrott

Women are called the opposite sex because when you want to do anything they want to do the opposite.

Corey Ford

Anyone making love to Germaine Greer should have his guide dog confiscated and be awarded the Victoria Cross.

Bernard Manning

It is relaxing to go out with my ex-wife because she already knows I'm an idiot.

Warren Thomas

I told my wife the truth. I told her I was seeing a psychiatrist. Then she told me the truth – she was seeing a psychiatrist, two plumbers and a bartender.

Rodney Dangerfield

Never marry a man with a big head. Because you're going to give birth to that man's child and you want a baby with a narrow head.

Jilly Goolden

A 'Bay Area Bisexual' told me I didn't quite coincide with either of her desires.

Woody Allen

Whatever else can be said about sex, it cannot be called a dignified performance.

Helen Lawrenson

I was so flat I used to put x's on my chest and write 'you are here'.

Joan Rivers

Zsa Zsa Gabor got married as a one-off and it was so successful she turned it into a series.

Bob Hope

My thirteenth wife cried and the judge wiped her tears with my chequebook.

Tommy Manville

I'm glad I'm not bisexual – I couldn't stand being rejected by men as well as women.

Bernard Manning

They kept mistresses of such dowdiness they might almost have been mistaken for wives.

Robertson Davies

'Tis better to have loved and lost than never to have lost at all.

Samuel Butler

There are three kinds of bachelors: the kind that must be driven into matrimony with a whip; the kind that must be coaxed with sugar; and the kind that must be blindfolded and backed into the shafts.

Helen Rowland

The only real argument for marriage is that it remains the best method for getting acquainted.

Heywood Brown

Alas! In choosing a husband, it seems that you've always got to decide between something tame and uninteresting, like a goldfish and something wild and fascinating like a mountain goat.

Helen Rowland

It is not true that I had nothing on. I had the radio on.

Marilyn Monroe

I feel cheated, never being able to know what it's like to get pregnant, carry a child and breastfeed.

Dustin Hoffman

My true friends have always given me that supreme proof of devotion; a spontaneous aversion for the man I loved.

Colette

When I'm good, I'm very very good, but when I'm bad, I'm better.

Mae West

I like to wake up feeling a new man.

Jean Harlow

The difference between a man and a woman I cannot conceive.

John Mahaffy

I was introduced to a beautiful young lady as a man in his nineties. Early nineties, I insisted.

George Burns

My girlfriend turns twenty-one next week. In honour of the event I'm going to stop bathing her in the sink.

Jerry Seinfeld

Women, You can't live with them and sheep can't cook.

Emo Philips

There's nothing like good food, good wine and a bad girl.

Robin Williams

I'm not a breast man. I'm a breast person.

John Wilson

I hate a woman who seems to be hermetically sealed in the lower regions.

H. Allen Smith

When a man makes a woman his wife, it's the highest compliment he can pay her, and it's usually the last.

Helen Rowland

Media and Films

Go see it and see for yourself why you shouldn't see it.

Sam Goldwyn

When people run up to me these days, it's not to ask for my autograph, but to get a closer look at my wrinkles.

Elizabeth Taylor

I have never appeared as a centrefold in *Playboy* because I couldn't stand a staple through my navel.

Diana Rigg

The cable TV sex channels don't expand our horizons, don't make us better people, and don't come in clearly enough.

Bill Maher

Television is probably the least physically harmful of all the narcotics known to man.

Christopher Lehmann-Haupt

Julie Andrews has lilacs instead of pubic hairs.

Christopher Plummer

There are two good reasons why men will go to see Jane Russell.

Howard Hughes

Don't say yes until I've finished talking.

Darryl F. Zanuck

After *The Wizard of Oz* I was typecast as a lion, and there aren't all that many parts for lions.

Bert Lahr

The Russians love Brooke Shields because her eyebrows remind them of Leonid Brezhnev.

Robin Williams

Have you ever noticed how the best acting at the Academy Awards ceremony is done by losers congratulating the winners?

George Roberts

An editor is a person employed by a newspaper, whose business it is to separate the wheat from the chaff, and to see that the chaff is printed.

Kin Hubbard

I would rather play Hamlet with no rehearsal than TV golf.

Jack Lemmon

I read the newspaper avidly. It is my one form of continuous fiction.

Aneurin Bevan

The policy of the British film censor would seem to be 'inner labia are out, but outer labia are in!'

Christopher Tookey

Take a good look at Keith Richards' face. He's turned into leather. He's a giant suitcase. He has a handle on his head. That's how they move him around at the concerts.

Denis Leary

You can never hope to become a skilled conversationalist until you learn how to put your foot tactfully through the television set.

Dale Baughman

In a national survey in Britain most people thought that Lulu the singer was fictitious and that Alf Garnett was real.

Warren Mitchell

We don't want the television script good – we want it Tuesday.

Dennis Norden

I have a face that is a cross between two pounds of halibut and an explosion in an old-clothes closet.

David Niven

The length of a film should be directly related to the endurance of the human bladder.

Alfred Hitchcock

You look at Ernest Borgnine and you think to yourself was there anybody else hurt in the accident?

Don Rickles

When I was a Sunday presenter on Classic FM I was not allowed to say goodbye to the listeners at the end of the programme in case they thought the station was closing down.

Tom Conti

Any movie that resorts to a talking tortise has serious problems.

Simon Rose

I'm all for a free press. It's the newspapers I can't stand.

Tom Stoppard

A James Cagney love scene is where he lets the other guy live.

Bob Hope

The mike boom appears more often in this film than some of the actors.

Simon Rose

As long as there are sex-mad teenagers swimming in the nude at night, there will be a *Friday the 13th* movie.

Simon Rose

Life doesn't imitate art – it imitates bad television.

Woody Allen

Lust in the Dust features the gargantuan transvestite Divine, with Hunter searching for some gold, guided only by a map that has been tatooed on a couple of pair of buttocks; sadly, after this refined start, it becomes rather cheap and tawdry.

Simon Rose

The best that can be said about Norwegian television is that it gives you the sensation of a coma without the worry and inconvenience.

Bill Bryson

This film cost $31 million. With that I could have invaded some country.

Clint Eastwood

It's the old old story. A diplomat's wife falls for a chimpanzee and is astounded at how stuffy and narrow-minded people can be.

Simon Rose

Depressingly, *Drop Dead Fred* became popular in America, but then so did serial killing.

Christopher Tookey

Burt Reynolds sings like Dean Martin with adenoids and dances like a drunk killing cockroaches.

John Barbour

George Mair was such a fastidious journalist, he once telephoned a semicolon from Moscow.

James Bone

My tears stuck in their little ducts, refusing to be jerked.

Peter Stack

People who are funny and smart and return phone calls get much better press than people who are just funny and smart.

Howard Simons

In Russia we had only two TV channels. Channel One was propaganda. Channel Two consisted of a KGB officer telling you, 'Turn back at once to Channel One.'

Yakov Smirnoff

In Hollywood, if you don't have happiness, you send out for it.

Rex Reed

Johnny, keep it out of focus. I want to win the foreign picture award.

Billy Wilder

In a moment, we hope to see the pole vault over the satellite.

David Coleman

Every director bites the hand that lays the golden egg.

Samuel Goldwyn

If it wasn't for Baird, the inventor of television, we'd still be eating frozen radio dinners.

Johnny Carson

It was once a rather half-hearted consumer programme, one of those don't-read-in-bed-with-a-blow-torch consumer progammes.

A.A. Gill

Animal rights activists demanded that the film-makers remove a scene in which a wolf attacks a man, describing it as an 'anti-wolf statement'.

Simon Rose

I cannot sing, dance or act – what else would I be but a talk-show host?

David Letterman

If you want to see a comic strip, you should see me in the shower.

Groucho Marx

Hollywood is the only place where an amicable divorce means each one gets fifty per cent of the publicity.

Lauren Bacall

Sean Connery's amazing array of accents includes Russian-Scottish, Irish-Scottish, Spanish-Scottish, Arabian-Scottish, and English-Scottish.

Simon Rose

Television's idea of an uplifting programme is one about brassieres.

Patrick Murray

I want you to put more life into your dying.

Samuel Goldwyn

John Ford shot a retake only if one of the horses misbehaved.

Maureen O'Hara

I'll give you a definite maybe.

Samuel Goldwyn

Cheech and Chong look like Abbot and Costello on drugs.

John Simon

How did I get to Hollywood? By train.

John Ford

My parents finally realise that I'm kidnapped and they snap into action immediately; they rent out my room.

Woody Allen

The worst movie I ever saw was *The Three Stooges Relax*.

Richard Lewis

Groucho isn't my real name – I'm just breaking it in for a friend.

Groucho Marx

Menabilly was full of dry rot. The only reason the building still stood was that the woodworm obligingly held hands.

Daphne Du Maurier

Bogart's a helluva nice guy until 10.30 p.m. After that he thinks he's Bogart.

David Chasen

Winning a Golden Rose of Montreux is a non-event because for as long as I can remember British Television has always won all of them. Even Hale and Pace got one, through in what category I can't begin to imagine. It must be so dispiriting being an Andorran comedy writer.

A.A. Gill

I don't have ulcers; I give them.

Harry Cahn

The career of Sylvester Stallone is more of a mystery than cot death.

Rex Reed

Epitaph for a Hollywood actress:
She Sleeps Alone At Last.

Robert Benchley

What do I think of Dustin Hoffman? It taught me never to work with any actor smaller than his Oscar.

Larry Gelbart

Sylvester Stallone's latest film *Cobra* is like being run over by a convoy of manure trucks.

Michael Pye

Let's have some new clichés.

Samuel Goldwyn

If Greta Garbo really wants to be alone, she should come to a performance of one of her films in Dublin.

Hugh Leonard

It's always been my ambition to go get hold of a video camera and to go round to Jeremy Beadle's house disguised as a mad axe-man, just for a laugh, and kill him.

Paul Merton

Journalists are people who take in another's washing and then sell it.

Marjorie Eldershaw

I didn't direct Mae West and W.C. Fields. I merely refereed the movie between them.

Eddie Cline

Film directors are people too short to become actors.

Josh Greenfield

Popcorn is the last area of the movie business where good taste is still a concern.

Mike Barfield

After Schwarzenegger, Dolph Lundgren is a bit of a disappointment. At least Arnie looks as if he comes supplied with batteries.

Adam Mars-Jones

A celebrity is any well-known TV or movie star who looks like he spends more than two hours working with his hair.

Steve Martin

The chat show is where a disc-jockey plays a few of his friends.

Frank Muir

In Hollywood, if a guy's wife looks like a new woman, she probably is.

Dean Martin

Having your book turned into a movie is like seeing your oxen turned into bouillon cubes.

John Le Carré

Women reporters are just trying to prove their manhood.

Ronald Reagan

I wish to be cremated. One tenth of my ashes shall be given to my agent, as written in our contract.

Groucho Marx

I've been accused of vulgarity. I say that's bullshit.

Mel Brooks

If the NBA was on Channel 5 and a bunch of frogs were making love on Channel 4 I'd watch the frogs, even if they were coming in fuzzy.

Bobby Knight

One day someone will join two Terry Christians together and make one long plank.

Rory Bremner

Elizabeth Taylor has more chins than the Chinese telephone directory.

Joan Rivers

I thought *Deep Throat* was a movie about a giraffe.

Bob Hope

Acting on television is like being asked by the captain to entertain the passengers while the ship goes down.

Peter Ustinov

A movie theatre manager in Seoul, South Korea, decided that the running time of *The Sound of Music* was too long. He shortened it by cutting out all the songs.

Bruce Felton

In Hollywood it's not enough to have a hit. Your best friend should also have a failure.

Peter Bogdanovich

My only advice to young actors is to stay out of jail.

Alfred Hitchcock

Hear no evil, see no evil and speak no evil – and you'll never get a job working for a tabloid.

Phil Pastoret

Raquel Welch is silicone fron the knees up.

George Masters

What do BBC weathermen do with their clothing allowance?

Mitchell Symons

A script of *Brideshead Revisited* needs an intravenous dose of syrup of figs or just a bullet.

A.A. Gill

It is a politician's right to refuse to speak to a journalist though he may afterwards find ways of penalising you.

Gerald Kaufman

The secret of successful journalism is to make your readers so angry they will write half your paper for you.

C.E.M. Joad

My grandfather and I used to sit for hours in front of the television watching it intently. Eventually he would say, 'Will we switch it on?'

Kevin McAleer

It is difficult to produce a television documentary that is both incisive and probing when every twelve minutes one is interrupted by twelve dancing rabbits singing about toilet paper.

R. Serlking

The one luxury I would take to a desert island is a television set that does not work.

Robert Mark

My movie *Assassins* is an existential action film – screenplay by Sartre and dialogue by Camus.

Sylvester Stallone

Every improvement in communication makes the bore more terrible.

Frank Moore Colby

Medicine and Doctors

The only people who have the right to use the editorial 'we' are presidents, editors and people with tapeworm.

Mark Twain

As she lay there dozing next to me, one voice inside my head kept saying, 'Relax, you are not the first doctor to sleep with one of his patients,' but another kept reminding me, 'Howard, you are a veterinarian.'

Dick Wilson

My teeth stuck out so far, I used to eat her kids' candy bars by accident.

Rita Rudner

The patient is not likely to recover who makes the doctor his heir.

Thomas Fuller

A mild heart attack is one you remember.

Jim Caffrey

It is a statistical fact that women who wear suspenders and stockings are less likely to suffer from gout, rickets or loneliness.

Craig Charles

Some people think you should eat human placenta because that's what animals do. Well, animals also lick their own balls. Do we have to do that too?

Denis Leary

My obstetrician was so dumb that when I gave birth he forgot to cut the cord. For a year that kid followed me everywhere. It was like having a dog on a leash.

Joan Rivers

Early to rise and early to bed,
Makes a male healthy, wealthy and dead.

James Thurber

Suicide is a real threat to health in a modern society.

Virginia Bottomley

A test for paranoia: if you cannot think of anything that's your fault, you've got it.

Robert Hutchins

If I had known I was going to live so long, I would have taken better care of myself.

George Burns

I cannot fight to the death, doctor's orders. I have an ulcer and dying is one of the worst things for it.

Woody Allen

Half of the patients who call the doctor in the middle of the night are suffering from wind.

Francis Young

My plastic surgeon told me my face looked like a bouquet of elbows.

Phyllis Diller

In the old days it was called voodoo and you used to stick needles into a doll. Now it is called acupuncture and you just stick them straight into the person.

Cathy Hopkins

The definition of an orthopaedic surgeon is someone with the strength of an ox but half the brain.

John Dorgan

Being ill is one of the greatest pleasures of life, provided one is not too ill and is not obliged to work until one is better.

Samuel Butler

I did consider liposuction at one point, but then I heard they can accidentally vacuum out internal organs that you're using.

Rita Rudner

Health nuts are going to feel stupid some day, lying in hospitals dying of nothing.

Red Foxx

It was not until I attended a few post-mortems that I realised that even the ugliest exteriors may contain the most beautiful viscera, and was able to console myself for the facial drabness of my neighbours in omnibuses by dissecting them in my imagination.

J.B.S. Haldene

Carl Llewellyn is so optimistic he would give himself a fifty-fifty chance after a decapitation.

Richard Edmondson

My dentist told me recently to spend more time with my gums.

Rita Rudner

Aneurin Bevan is a thrombosis – a bloody clot that undermines the constitution.

Winston Churchill

Whenever I fill in an application, it says 'In case of emergency, notify ...'. I put 'Doctor'. What the hell would my mother do in an emergency?

Steven Wright

Dying can damage your health. Every coffin contains a Government Health Warning.

Spike Milligan

The last time I saw anything like you, the whole herd had to be destroyed.

Eric Morecambe

The practice of medicine is a thinker's art, the practice of surgery a plumber's.

Martin Fischer

These modern analysts, they charge so much. In my day for five marks Freud himself would treat you. For ten marks he would treat you and press your pants. For fifteen marks Freud would let you treat him – that included a choice of any two vegetables.

Woody Allen

Blood! That should be on the inside.

Woody Allen

One of the minor pleasures of life is to be slightly ill.

Harold Nicholson

I've been smoking for thirty years now and there's nothing wrong with my lung.

Freddie Starr

I learned why they are called wonder drugs – you wonder what they'll do to you.

Harlan Miller

People wish their enemies dead, but I do not; I say give them the gout, give them the stone!

Mary Montagu

It requires a great deal of faith for a man to be cured by his own placebos.

John McClenahan

Garry Maddox has turned his life around. He used to be depressed and miserable. Now he's miserable and depressed.

Harry Kalas

No one can feel as helpless as the owner of a sick goldfish.

Kin Hubbard

I refused to have an operation on the grounds that I already had two operations and found them painful. They were having my hair cut and sitting for my portrait.

Richard Brinsley Sheridan

In hospital, bleeding to death takes second place to filling in forms.

Bill Dana

Cystitis is a living death, it really is. Nobody ever talks about it, but if I was faced with a choice between having my arms removed and getting cystitis, I'd wave goodbye to my arms quite happily.

Louise Wesner

A bottle of sleeping tablets I have just bought bears the label 'WARNING – MAY CAUSE DROWSINESS'.

Peter Orr

My genitals are like a sort of travel version of Linford Christie's.

Frank Skinner

I'm not as normal as I appear.

Woody Allen

Physicians of the Utmost Fame
Were called at once, but when they came
They answered, as they took their fees,
'There is no cure for this disease.'

Hilaire Belloc

Physicians of all men are most happy; what good success soever they have, the world proclaimeth, and what faults they commit, the earth covereth.

Francis Quarles

No doctor takes pleasure in the health even of his friends.

Montaigne

To really really lose weight playing golf, the best place to play is Mexico. Go to any Mexican golf course, stop at every hole, and drink water. Within a week you'll be down to your desired weight.

Buddy Hackett

The trouble with being a hypochondriac these days is that antibiotics have cured all the good diseases.

Caskie Stinnet

Boot's cough syrup for children bears a notice saying DO NOT DRIVE CAR OR OPERATE MACHINERY. AVOID ALCOHOLIC DRINKS.

Robin Young

Advice to expectant mothers: you must remember that when you are pregnant, you are eating for two. But you must remember that the other one of you is about the size of a golf ball, so let's not go overboard with it. A lot of pregnant women eat as though the other person they're eating for is Orson Welles.

Dave Barry

The genitals themselves have not undergone the development of the rest of the human form in the direction of beauty.

Sigmund Freud

It's a good idea to obey all the rules when you're young just so you'll have the strength to break them when you're old.

Mark Twain

Exercise is just a short cut to the cemetery.

John Mortimer

Here is a health warning: be suspicious of any doctor who tries to take your temperature with his finger.

David Letterman

Tell me your phobias and I'll tell you what you're afraid of.

Robert Benchley

I was in analysis for years because of a traumatic childhood; I was breast-fed through falsies.

Woody Allen

People who feel well are sick people neglecting themselves.

Jules Romains

When I go to the dentist, he's the one that has to have the anaesthetic.

Phyllis Diller

Medicine and Doctors

When I was forty my doctor advised me that a man in his forties shouldn't play tennis. I heeded his advice carefully and could hardly wait until I reached fifty to start again.

Hugo Black

First the doctor told me the good news – I was going to have a disease named after me.

Steve Martin

Music

I can't open my eyes when I'm singing because the words are
written on the back of my eyelids.

Christy Moore

I went to watch Pavarotti once. He doesn't like it when you
join in.

Mick Miller

I can't listen to that much Wagner. I start getting the urge to
conquer Poland.

Woody Allen

Madame, I have cried only twice in my life; once when I
dropped a wing of truffled chicken into Lake Como, and
once when for the first time I heard you sing.

Gioacchino Rossini

I don't think the orchestra as we know it will survive. The
future lies with the chamber orchestra of highly professional
soloids.

Thomas Beecham

I bought an audio cleaning tape. I'm a big fan of theirs.

Kevin Gildea

A trombone is a quaint and antique drainage system applied
to the face.

Thomas Beecham

Modern music is just noise with attitude.

Patrick Murray

Jerry Lee Lewis has been married twenty times. He gets married on a Tuesday, they find his wife dead in a swimming pool on Thursday. Maybe if you married someone who's old enough to swim next time, OK Jerry?

Denis Leary

I like to conduct ballet music at a very fast tempo. That makes the buggers hop.

Thomas Beecham

A piano is a piano is a piano.

Gertrude Steinway

Talking of Toscanini, I hear he is in some trouble with his eyes and has therefore to conduct from memory. It is indeed a double affliction when you consider how many years he has been practically tone-deaf.

Thomas Beecham

The upright piano is a musical growth found adhering to the walls of most semi-detached houses in the provinces.

Thomas Beecham

I am a rock music producer. It is an honour and a privilege to be in the same business as Wagner and Elgar.

Pete Waterman

I love Wagner, but the music I prefer is that of a cat hung up by its tail outside a window and trying to stick to panes of glass with its claws.

Charles Baudelaire

Going to the opera, like getting drunk, is a sin that carries its own punishment with it.

Hannah More

Jazz is the most degraded form of human aberration.

Thomas Beecham

If a literary man puts together two words about music, one of them will be wrong.

Aaron Copland

The singers think they are going to be heard. It is the duty of the orchestra to make sure they are not.

Thomas Beecham

I know two kinds of audience only – one coughing and one not coughing.

Artur Schnabel

The harpsichord is a birdcage played with a toasting fork.

Thomas Beecham

Of course we've all dreamed of reviving the castrati and I have drawn up a list of well-known singers I'm sure would benefit. It's only a matter of getting them to agree.

Henry Reed

No opera plot can be sensible for in sensible situations people do not sing.

W.H. Auden

I am very fond of women, but in an orchestra if they're not good-looking – and often they're not and they always look worse when they're blowing – it puts me off, while if they are good-looking it puts me off a damn sight more.

Thomas Beecham

There's a fellow, John Lennon. He wanted peace and he got it.

Bernard Manning

I have just seen Niagara Falls – fortissimo at last.

Gustav Mahler

All music is folk music – I ain't ever heard no horse sing.

Louis Armstrong

Because of its famous echo, British composers should all endeavour to have their works performed in the Royal Albert Hall; they will thus be assured of at least two performances.

Thomas Beecham

The concert is a polite form of self-imposed torture.

Henry Miller

How is it possible for Bob Dylan to play the harmonica, professionally, for thirty years and still show no sign of improvement?

David Sinclair

The organ of Winchester Cathedral is audible at five miles, painful at three, and lethal at one.

Thomas Beecham

Ladies and gentlemen, in upwards of fifty years of concert-giving, it has seldom been my good fortune to find the programme correctly printed. Tonight is no exception to the rule, and therefore, with your kind permission, we will now play you the piece which you think you have just heard.

Thomas Beecham

A piano is a parlour utensil for subduing the impenitent visitor. It is operated by depressing the keys of the machine and the spirits of the audience.

Ambrose Bierce

Harpists spend half their life tuning and the other half playing out of tune.

Thomas Beecham

Every supermarket has a dungeon housing a staff of deaf and dumb troglodytes especially trained to make random selections of cassettes for playing during business hours.

George Crosby

When you have nothing to say, sing it.

David Ogilvy

Can't you read? The score demands *con amore*, and what are you doing? You are playing it like married men.

Arturo Toscanini

The difference between a bass and a cello is that a bass burns longer.

Thomas Beecham

He was a fiddler and consequently a rogue.

Jonathan Swift

My biggest regret in life is that I didn't hit John Denver in the mouth while I had the chance.

Denis Leary

Michael Jackson looks like a Barbie doll that has been whittled by a malicious brother.

Thomas Sutcliffe

Once you're dead, you're made for life.

Jimi Hendrix

 **Music**

Mick Jagger is about as sexy as a pissing toad.

Truman Capote

Cole Porter sang like a hinge.

Ethel Merman

How thankful we ought to feel that Wordsworth was only a poet and not a musician. Fancy a symphony by Wordsworth! Fancy having to sit it out! And fancy what it would have been if he had written fugues!

Samuel Butler

Bernstein uses music merely as an accompaniment to his conducting.

Oscar Levant

All the good music has already been written by people with wigs and stuff.

Frank Zappa

Frank Sinatra's game is fine – but I still prefer golf.

Arnold Palmer

The approach of Frankie Lane to the microphone is that of an accused man pleading with a hostile jury.

Kenneth Tynan

A homeless musician is one without a girlfriend.

Dave Barry

It's bad when they don't perform your operas – but when they do, it's far worse.

Camille Saint-Saëns

I spent many years laughing at Harry Secombe's singing until somebody told me it wasn't a joke.

Spike Milligan

The *Glasgow Herald* once carried a classified ad which read 'Bagpipes, used only once, for sale, owing to bereavement.'

Billy Connolly

For three hundred years flautists tried to play in tune. Then they gave up and invented vibrato.

George Barrère

The Sydney Opera House looks like a typewriter full of oyster shells, like a broken Pyrex casserole dish in a brown cardboard box.

Clive James

If only James had stuck to music, we might have made some money.

Nora Joyce

I don't like piccolo playing even if it's good.

Franklin P. Adams

 **Music**

When conducting an orchestra, if you as much as look at the brass instruments, they will play too loudly.

Richard Strauss

Australia was the first country not to require that women play the cello side-saddle.

John Thompson

They all laughed when I sat down at the piano, but oh!, when I began to play, they laughed even more.

John Caples

The typewriting machine, when played with expression is no more annoying than the piano when played by a sister or near relation.

Oscar Wilde

Nationalities and Places

Gaiety is the most outstanding feature of the Soviet Union.

Joseph Stalin

I once stayed in a German hotel which displayed the notice
BREAKFAST IST OBLIGATORY.

Derek Nimmo

This Scottish fellow had a hip replacement operation. He
asked the surgeon if he could have the bone for his dog.

Frank Carson

Of course, travelling is much easier today than it used to be.
A hundred years ago, it could take you the better part of a
year to get from New York to California; whereas today,
because of equipment problems at O'Hare, you can't get
there at all.

Dave Barry

I went to Naples to see Vesuvius and would you believe it,
the bloody fools had let it go out.

Spike Milligan

A Dublin marriage proposal often goes like this: would ya
like to go halves on a baby?

Brendan Behan

I like the Irish but I cannot quite understand how when I say
'I'm from London', in a Dublin pub, this tends to be heard as
'I am Oliver Cromwell'.

Jo Brand

The English may not like music, but they absolutely love the noise it makes.

Thomas Beecham

In Anglo-Saxon countries men prefer the company of other men. In England twenty-five per cent of the men are homosexual.

Edith Cresson

New York City is perfectly safe if you follow certain commonsense safety rules such as:
1 Always walk at at least 30 miles per hour
2 Always keep your money and other valuables in a safe place, such as Switzerland
3 Avoid unsafe areas, such as your hotel bedroom
4 Never make eye contact. This is asking to be mugged. In the New York court system, a mugger is automatically declared not guilty if the defence can prove the victim has a history of making eye contact.

Dave Barry

In Ethiopia when a father turns to his son and says, 'Whaddya want to do when you grow up?' nine times out of ten the kid says 'Eat'.

Denis Leary

I don't like abroad. I've been there.

King George V

I am not wanting to make too long speech tonight as I am knowing your old English saying 'Early to bed and up with the cock!'

Yakov Smirnoff

I saw the new Italian navy. Its boats have glass bottoms so they can see the old Italian navy.

Peter Secchia

An Iranian moderate is one who has run out of ammunition.

Henry Kissinger

The Race Relations Board concentrated their fire some years ago on a fellow who was selling Irish coffee mugs which had the handle on the inside. He turned out to be a native of Cork.

Stan Gebler Davies

We had gone out there to pass the beautiful day of high summer like true Irishmen – locked in the dark snug of a public house.

Brendan Behan

Poland is now a totally independent nation, and it has managed to greatly improve its lifestyle thanks to the introduction of modern Western conveniences such as food.

Dave Barry

Waiting for the verb in German is the ultimate thrill.

Flann O'Brien

The Swiss are not a people so much as a neat, clean, quite solvent business.

William Faulkner

It profits a man nothing to give his soul for the whole world – but for Wales?

Thomas More

The Germans – if they can't stuff it into an animal casing they won't eat it.

Tim Allen

There must be at least 500 million rats in the United States; of course, I am speaking only from memory.

Edgar W. Nye

My mind is like a Welsh railway – one track and dirty.

Dylan Thomas

When asked by an anthropologist what the Indians called America before the white man came, an Indian said simply 'Ours'.

Vine Deloira

Eating in Germany is easy because there is basically only one kind of food, called the 'wurst'. This is a delicious item made by compressing random pig parts until they have reached the density of bowling balls, then serving them in long brown units that don't look at all like large bowel movements, so just put that thought right out of your mind.

Dave Barry

On entering the United States I was given a form to fill in by the Immigration Authority. To the question 'Is it your intention to overthrow the government of the US by force', I gave the written answer 'Sole purpose of visit'.

Gilbert Harding

The English are a pacifist race – they always hold their wars in someone else's country.

Brendan Behan

England were beaten only in the sense that they lost.

Dickie Davis

England had Thatcher. We had Reagan. But at least we have one thing we can hold over England's head. We tried to kill Reagan.

Denis Leary

The Englishwoman is so refined.
She has no bosom and no behind.

Stevie Smith

In Ireland schizophrenics are treated not by one psychiatrist but by two.

Barry Took

German is a language which was developed solely to afford the speaker the opportunity to spit at strangers under the guise of polite conversation.

P.J. O'Rourke

If I were a cassowary
On the plains of Timbuctoo,
I would eat a missionary
Cassock, band, and hymn-book too.

Samuel Wilberforce

Poor Mexico, so far from God and so close to the United States.

Porfiris Diaz

A Russian and a Polish labourer repairing a derelict house chanced upon a horde of gold. The Russian said eagerly 'We will share it like brothers'. 'No,' replied the Pole, 'fifty-fifty'.

Peter Ustinov

Practically every game played internationally today was invented in Britain, and when foreigners became good enough to match or even defeat the British, the British quickly invented a new game.

Peter Ustinov

In a restaurant, the average Englishman would much prefer poor food, poor service and a good complaint to the manager and maybe even a letter to the *Times* rather than enjoy a good meal.

Malcolm Muggeridge

Montreal is the only place on earth where a good French accent isn't a social asset.

Brendan Behan

The Welsh have overrun the country with nonconformity and lust.

Evelyn Waugh

Here is the difference between Dante, Milton and me. They wrote about Hell and never saw the place. I wrote about Chicago after looking the town over for years and years.

Carl Sandburg

Lichtenstein and Luxembourg are not European nations. They are minor characters in William Shakespeare's famous play Hamlet II: The Next Day.

Dave Barry

I went to the United States for one purpose only; to continue my lifelong search for naked women in wet mackintoshes.

Dylan Thomas

She's not dead sir, she's English.

Cathy Hopkins

The French are sawed-off sissies who eat snails and slugs and cheese that smells like people's feet. They are utter cowards who force their own children to drink wine and they gibber like baboons even when you try to speak to them in their own wimpy language.

P.J. O'Rourke

New Zealanders will bet on anything that moves, and, if it doesn't move, they will kick it and bet on when it will move.

Robin Oakley

Californication.

James Montgomery

Americans will put up with anything provided it doesn't block traffic.

Dan Rather

Last week I went to Philadelphia, but it was closed.

W.C. Fields

Natives who beat drums to drive off evil spirits are objects of scorn to Americans who blow horns to break up traffic jams.

Mary Ellen Kelly

There is nothing at all primitive about European medical care except that in some countries they practise it in foreign languages, meaning you run the risk of entering hospital complaining of an inflamed appendix and coming out as a member of a completely different gender.

Dave Barry

One of the cardinal rules of travel is 'stay the hell out of Paraguay'.

Dave Barry

The French and the English are such good enemies that they can't resist being friends.

Peter Ustinov

My father never lived to see his dream come true of an all Yiddish-speaking Canada.

David Steinberg

If you are not in New York you are camping out.

Thomas Dewing

The Spanish Civil War was not a war at all. It was a comic opera with an occasional death.

Georges Kopp

Texas used to be the largest state, but because of Alaska, it no longer is. Texans are still very touchy about this, so you should be sensitive when you discuss it with them. 'What a large state this is, despite being nowhere near as large as Alaska!', is a sensitive remark you might want to make.

Dave Barry

Two out of five Irish women prefer alcohol to sex and it's just my luck to have gone out with both of them.

Joseph O'Connor

The Germans are a cruel race. Their operas last for six hours and they have no word for fluffy.

Rowan Atkinson

Scotsmen wear kilts because sheep can hear zippers a mile away.

Blanche Knott

You can have no concept of the vastness and emptines of the outback of Australia until you have seen the dress circle of a Sydney theatre on a Saturday afternoon.

Robert Morley

'Vacation' is the word Americans use to describe going someplace different to have fun and get away from all their trials and tribulations. The English call it 'holiday'. In Russia it's known as 'defecting'.

Yakov Smirnoff

Many people are surprised to hear we have comedians in Russia, but they are there. They are dead, but they are there.

Yakov Smirnoff

I have recently been all round the world and have formed a very poor opinion of it.

Thomas Beecham

Finland has produced so many brilliant distance runners because back home it costs $2.50 a gallon for gas.

Esa Tikkannery

John Kenneth Galbraith and Marshall McLuhan are the two greatest modern Canadians that the US has produced.

Anthony Burgess

I have just returned from a weekend in Paris and all I can say is that sex in Ireland is only in its infancy.

Patrick Kavanagh

The Welsh are said to be so remarkably fond of cheese, that in cases of difficulty their midwives apply a piece of toasted cheese to the *janua vitae* to attract and entice the young Taffy, who on smelling it makes the most vigorous efforts to come forth.

Francis Grose

There's a store in New York called Bonjour Croissant. It makes me want to go to Paris and open a store called Hello Toast.

Fran Lebowitz

Hoover's slogan was 'a chicken in every pot' but Gorbachev has a new slogan: a chicken in every time zone.

Johnny Carson

These two Irishmen were passing a pub – well it could happen.

Frank Carson

We are now approaching Belfast Airport. Please fasten your seatbelts, extinguish your cigarettes and put your watches back three hundred years.

Niall Toibin

I had this prejudice against the British until I discovered half of them were female.

Ray Floyd

An Englishman, even if he is quite alone, forms an orderly queue of one.

George Mikes

The English instinctively admire any man who has no talent and is modest about it.

James Agee

My first rule of travel is never to go to a place that sounds like a medical condition and Critz is clearly an incurable disease involving flaking skin.

Bill Bryson

Everything you ever need to know about the Germans' innate sense of romance, lyricism, eroticism and indeed their tender feelings for the fairer sex is encapsulated in their word for nipple. The German word is *brustwarze*, a breast wart.

A.A. Gill

I am moving to Switzerland because I am devoted to chocolate.

Noel Coward

Intelligence governs our universe except in certain parts of New Jersey.

Woody Allen

Another innocent bystander was shot in New York yesterday. You just stand around in this town long enough and be innocent and somebody is going to shoot you.

Will Rogers

What annoys me about Britain is the rugged will to lose.

William Camp

Beautiful city of Glasgow I now conclude my muse,
And to write in praise of thee my pen does not refuse;
And, without fear of contradiction, I will venture to say
You are the second grandest city in Scotland at the present day.

William McGonagall

Britain has invented a new missile. It's called the civil servant – it doesn't work and it can't be fired.

Walter Walker

A gifted person ought to learn English (barring spelling and pronouncing) in thirty hours, French in thirty days, and German in thirty years.

Mark Twain

Niagara Falls is simply a vast unnecessary amount of water going the wrong way and then falling over unnecessary rocks.

Oscar Wilde

An Irishman will always soften bad news, so that a major coronary is no more than 'a bad turn', and a near-hurricane that leaves thousands homeless is 'good drying weather'.

Hugh Leonard

All culture corrupts, but French culture corrupts absolutely.

Laurence Durrell

In the Dublin of the 1930s to get enough to eat was regarded as an achievement. To get drunk was a victory.

Brendan Behan

The two sides of industry have traditionally always regarded each other in Britain with the greatest possible loathing, mistrust and contempt. They are both absolutely right.

Auberon Waugh

In America you can always find a party. In Russia, the party always finds you.

Yakov Smirnoff

One thing I will say for the Germans, they are always perfectly willing to give anybody's land to somebody else.

Will Rogers

Lord I will go wherever you want me to. But not India.

St Thomas

Only one arrest was made at the Belgium v. Ireland match in Brussels. It was an Irishman with a painted moustache who attempted to kiss a police horse.

Patrick Murray

The great thing about Glasgow now is that if there's a nuclear attack it'll look exactly the same afterwards.

Billy Connolly

I see the customs authorities in England searched the round-the-world fliers when they landed. I guess they thought the boys had smuggled over a couple of baby grand pianos.

Will Rogers

You always know a sick Irishman is on the mend when you see him blowing the froth off his medicine.

Brendan Behan

Thery'll always be an England, even if it's in Hollywood.

Bob Hope

The Irish are excellent timekeepers because they are used to working with watches that are an hour fast and ten minutes slow.

Patrick Murray

The English think that incompetence is the same thing as sincerity.

Quentin Crisp

To hear a German struggling with language is like watching a deep sea diver disappearing under the water before finally emerging with the verb between his teeth.

Mark Twain

Saloons in Philadelphia were closed at twelve o'clock on Saturday night and opened at one minute past midnight on Sunday.

W.C. Fields

Three ducks were flying over Belfast. The first duck said
'quack', the second duck said 'quack' and the third duck said
'Look, I'm going as quack as I can'.

Frank Carson

It is part of the unwritten British Constitution that all major
events have to be presented by a Dimbleby.

Jeremy Paxman

He created a man who was hard of head, blunt of speech,
knew which side his bread was buttered on, and above all
took no notice of women. Then God sent him forth to
multiply in Yorkshire.

Reginald Hill

Polar exploration is at once the cleanest and most isolated
way of having a bad time which has been devised.

Apsley Cherry-Garrard

The importance of a country is inversely proportional to the
length of its national anthem.

Allen Otter

All Englishmen talk as if they've got a bushel of plums stuck
in their throats, and then after swallowing them get
constipated from the pits.

W.C. Fields

Nationalities and Places

Of all noxious animals, the most noxious is a tourist. And of all tourists, the most vulgar, ill-bred, offensive and loathsome is the British tourist.

Francis Kilvert

What I look forward to most on returning from a long tour of India is a dry fart.

Phil Edmunds

In parts of India they have a law that if a man is married and is unfaithful to his wife, her family can take him out and publicly shoot him. There is no trial or anything – it's just their religious and state custom. If that was the custom in America, I would take every cent I make and put it into an ammunition factory.

Will Rogers

I do not dislike the French for their vulgar antipathy between neighbouring nations, but for their insolent and unfounded airs of superiority.

Horace Walpole

In an underdeveloped country, don't drink the water; in a developed country, don't breathe the air.

Jonathan Raban

Italian men and Russian women don't shave before a race.

Eddy Ottoz

The Irish treat you like royalty before and after a game, and kick you to pieces during it.

Jeff Probyn

French bread is so long so they can dip it in the sewer.

Blanche Knott

On my first day in New York a guy asked me if I knew where Central Park was. When I told him I didn't he said, 'Do you mind if I mug you here?'

Paul Merton

I bought a Korean kitchen knife. The label read: WARNING – KEEP OUT OF CHILDREN.

Robin Young

I was in a pub in Glasgow the other night. What a rough joint it was – they had a pig on the counter as an air freshener.

Stan Boardman

They say if you stop smoking you'll get your sense of smell back. I live in New York City – why do I want my sense of smell back?

Bill Hicks

Have you heard about the Irishman who reversed into a car boot sale and sold the engine?

Frank Carson

A motto for New Jersey – Not as bad as you might have expected.

Calvin Trillin

We used to play a game in Liverpool called forwards, backwards, sideways. You'd hit a fellow on the head with a shovel and guess which way he'd fall.

Stan Beardman

Foreign tourists should realise that in England they are encouraged to take a piece of fruit, free of charge, from any open-air stall or display.

Michael Lipton

I don't mind dictatorships abroad provided they are pro-American.

George Wallace

In the Soviet Army it takes more courage to retreat than to advance.

Joseph Stalin

The only English words I saw in Japan were Sony and Mitsubishi.

Bill Gullickson

Boy George is all England needs: another Queen who can't dress.

Joan Rivers

I hate two towns. Edmonton and Aswan. I've enjoyed all the rest. Even New Zealand.

John Cleese

Visitors to England should be informed that London barbers are delighted to shave patrons' armpits.

Gerard Hoffnung

An Aborigine is a non-speaking character actor in an Australian movie.

Mike Barfield

I swear I saw a road sign in Ireland which said: WARNING! THIS IS A ONE WAY CUL-DE-SAC AT BOTH ENDS.

Spike Milligan

A Canadian is someone who knows how to make love in a canoe.

Pierre Berton

Boy, those French – they have a different word for everything.

Steve Martin

The curtain rises on a vast primitive wasteland, not unlike certain parts of New Jersey.

Woody Allen

The Middle Eastern states aren't nations; they're quarrels with borders.

P.J. O'Rourke

My dear Oscar, you are not clever enough for us in Dublin. You had better run over to Oxford.

John Mahaffy

Very big, China.

Noel Coward

It was wonderful to find America, but it would have been still more wonderful to miss it.

Mark Twain

France has neither winter nor summer nor morals – apart from these drawbacks it is a fine country.

Mark Twain

Welsh Nationalists are a political group successful in having secured extra work for indigenous traffic-sign writers.

Mike Barfield

A family of my acquaintance in Glasgow had their father badly burnt in a fire so they demanded half price at the crematorium.

Michael Munro

Since both of Switzerland's national products, snow and chocolate, melt, the cuckoo clock was invented solely in order to give tourists something solid to remember it by.

Alan Coren

I think one of the highest compliments ever paid to Australia was the imminent Japanese invasion. To think the Japanese would actually think of coming to Australia to live! They did change their mind, with a little persuasion.

Barry Humphries

Politics

It is no exaggeration to say that the undecideds could go one way or the other.

George Bush

I've read about foreign policy and studied – I know a number of continents.

George Wallace

It was but a few weeks since he had taken his seat in the House of Lords; and this afternoon, for want of anything better to do, he strayed in and sat in it.

Max Beerbohm

Thank God W.C. Fields was a comic. Had he been a statesman he would have plunged the world into total war.

Will Rogers

We'd all like to vote for the best man but he's never a candidate.

Kin Hubbard

In 1932 President Herbert Hoover was so desperate to remain in the White House that he dressed up as Eleanor Roosevelt. When FDR discovered the hoax in 1936, the two men decided to stay together for the sake of the children.

Johnny Carson

Consider the Vice-President, George Bush, a man so
bedevilled by bladder problems that he managed, for the last
eight years, to be in the men's room whenever an important
illegal decision was made.

Barbara Ehrenreich

We expect the Salvadorean officials to work towards the
extermination of human rights.

Dan Quayle

Hey you guys, get up! Reagan is President. Call the Betty
Ford Centre. We shoulda known, man. They let us do all the
drugs and have unlimited sex so we would forget to vote.
They caught us with our pants down.

Denis Leary

Do you remember the good old days when sleeping with
the President meant you attended a cabinet meeting?

P.J. O'Rourke

Members of Parliament are the blind leading the people who
can see.

G.K. Chesterton

Gerald Ford can't fart and chew gum at the same time.

Lyndon B. Johnson

I can think of no better step to signalise the inauguration of the National Health Service than that Aneurin Bevan who so obviously needs psychiatric attention should be among the first of its patients.

Winston Churchill

The War Office kept three sets of figures; one to mislead the public, another to mislead the Cabinet and a third to mislead itself.

H.H. Asquith

The only safe pleasure for a member of parliament nowadays is a bag of boiled sweets.

Julian Critchley

I have opinions of my own – strong opinions – but I don't always agree with them.

George Bush

Let the Democratic Party try winning and see what it feels like. If we don't like it, we can go back to our traditions.

Paul Tsongas

Any political party that includes the word 'democratic' in its name, isn't.

Patrick Murray

For twenty years Herbert Asquith has held a season ticket on the line of least resistance and has gone wherever the train of events has carried him, lucidly justifying his position at whatever point he has happened to find himself.

Leo Amery

If capitalism depended on the intellectual quality of the Conservative Party, it would end about lunchtime tomorrow.

Tony Benn

Sir Anthony Eden was half mad baronet and half beautiful woman.

R.A. Butler

The quickest way to become a left winger in the Labour Party today is to stand still for six months.

Dave Nellist

Any American citizen can become President of the United States, just as long as he's a millionaire.

Patrick Murray

Margaret Thatcher went to Venice only because somebody told her she could walk down the middle of the street.

Neil Kinnock

No man is regular in his attendance at the House of Commons until he is married.

Benjamin Disraeli

We shoot JFK, we shoot RFK but when it comes to Teddy we go, 'Ah, leave him alone, he'll screw it up himself, no problem, you know'. He's the biggest target in the whole goddamn Kennedy family – and nobody takes a shot at him. He weighs about 7,000 pounds. You could shoot a bullet in Los Angeles and hit him in the ass in Boston five minutes later.'

Denis Leary

Never believe anything in politics until it has been officially denied.

Otto Von Bismarck

Corruption is nature's way of restoring our faith in democracy.

Peter Ustinov

Anybody who enjoys being in the House of Commons probably needs psychiatric help.

Ken Livingstone

The typical Socialist is a prim little man with a white-collar job, usually a secret teetotaller and often with vegetarian leanings, with a history of Nonconformity behind him, and, above all, with a social position which he has no intention of forfeiting.

George Orwell

There were so many candidates on the Democratic platform that there were not enough promises to go round.

Ronald Reagan

Ronald Reagan doesn't dye his hair, he's just prematurely orange.

Gerald Ford

The peace process is like a wedding night in a minefield.

Shimon Peres

I am not a politician, and my other habits are good.

Artemus Ward

Trust J. Edgar Hoover as much as you would a rattlesnake with a silencer on its rattle.

Dean Acheson

Most British statesmen have either drunk too much or womanised too much. I never fell into the second category.

George Brown

How the hell would I know why there were Nazis? I don't even know how a can opener works.

Woody Allen

I hope I stand for anti-bigotry, anti-racism and anti-Semitism.

George Bush

The President is going to lead us out of this recovery.

Dan Quayle

Politics

Tony Blair has pushed moderation to extremes.

Robert MacLennan

An election is coming. Universal peace is declared, and the foxes have a sincere interest in prolonging the lives of the poultry.

George Eliot

The members of Congress never open their mouths without subtracting from the sum of human knowledge.

Thomas Reed

At the reunion at a Washington party a few weeks ago there were three ex-Presidents, Carter, Ford and Nixon: See no Evil, Hear no Evil and Evil.

Bob Dole

My dog Millie knows more about foreign policy than those two bozos Clinton and Gore.

George Bush

In a democracy everyone has the right to be represented, including the jerks.

Chris Patten

The world 'liberty' in the mouth of Daniel Webster is like the word 'love' in the mouth of a courtesan.

Ralph Waldo Emerson

Facts are stupid things.

Ronald Reagan

A politician is an arse upon which everyone has sat except a man.

e.e. cummings

Calvin Coolidge slept more than any other President, whether by day or by night. Nero fiddled, but Coolidge only snored.

H.L. Mencken

I have always said about Tony Benn that he immatures with age.

Harold Wilson

People that are really very weird can get into sensitive positions and have a tremendous impact on history.

Dan Quayle

Politics would be a helluva good business if it weren't for the goddamned people.

Richard Nixon

It's not the voting that's democracy, it's the counting.

Tom Stoppard

Haven't we got all the fools in town on our side? And ain't that a big enough majority in any town?

Mark Twain

The House of Commons is the longest running farce in the West End.

Cyril Smith

President Johnson was a real centaur – part man and part horse's ass.

Dean Acheson

The largest turnout at elections is always where there is only one candidtate.

Peter Ustinov

That one never asks a question unless he knows the answer is basic to parliamentary questioning.

John Diefenbaker

You might be interested to know that the scriptures are on our side in relation to the arms build-up.

Ronald Reagan

Sir Anthony Eden was not only a bore; he bored for England.

Malcolm Muggeridge

It is often said that the central lobby in the House of Commons is the third easiest place in Europe to pick people up after Funland in Leicester Square and the arrival lounge at Rome airport.

Alan Clark

Winston Churchill devoted the best years of his life to preparing his impromptu speeches.

F.E. Smith

Joseph McCarthy is the only major politician in the country who can be labelled 'liar' without fear of libel.

Joseph Alsop

Politicians are interested in people in the same way that dogs are interested in fleas.

P.J. O'Rourke

No diet will remove all the fat from your body because the brain is entirely fat. Without a brain you might look good, but all you could do is run for public office.

Covert Bailey

I have nothing against Kinnock. I just think it's a shame her husband is such a spineless dork.

Kit Hollerbach

I enjoy American political debates more than Soviet political debates because there are twice as many people involved – two instead of one.

Yakov Smirnoff

In the US Civil War, they were cutting each other's throats because one half of them prefer hiring their servants for life, and the other by the hour.

Thomas Carlyle

Most politicians look like people who have become human by correspondence course.

A.A. Gill

Giving money and power to the government is like giving whiskey and car keys to teenage boys.

P.J. O'Rourke

No man ever listened himself out of a job.

Calvin Coolidge

If elected, I will win.

Pat Paulsen

Why talk with the monkey when you can talk with the organ grinder?

Winston Churchill

Nothing was ever done so systematically as nothing is being done now.

Woodrow Wilson

I wear the pants in our house but I also wash and iron them.

Denis Thatcher

The House of Lords is a second chamber elected by the whips – a seraglio of eunuchs.

Michael Foot

I will sit on the fence if it is strong enough.

Cyril Smith

When Henry Kissinger won the Nobel Peace Prize, I gave up satire on grounds of unfair competition.

Tom Lehrer

The ship of state is the only known vessel that leaks from the top.

James Reston

They say everyone remembers what he was doing when Kennedy was shot. I'd love to ask Lee Harvey Oswald what he was doing.

Paul Merton

I can always tell how well I stand politically by the number of fingers Lady Londonderry offers me at her receptions.

Austin Chamberlain

Who drinks more, the House or the Senate? I believe the House drinks more because it has 531 members and the Senate has only 96. But if the Senate had about two more members they would go ahead of them.

Will Rogers

Who is responsible for the riots? The rioters!

Dan Quayle

When Clinton says 'Attorney General', he means the first semi-qualified woman he could find without a criminal record.

Mort Sahl

I can't say I've ever got visually, artistically or sexually excited by any of the women MPs. They all look as though they're from the Fifth Kiev Stalinist machine-gun parade.

Nicholas Fairbairn

Frankly, I'd like to see the government get out of war altogether and leave the whole field to private industry.

Joseph Heller

That son of a bitch MacArthur isn't going to resign on me. I want him fired.

Harry S. Truman

Henry VIII perhaps approached as nearly to the ideal standard of perfect wickedness as the infirmities of human nature will allow.

James Mackintosh

Margaret Beckett looks like a woman resigned to walk home alone to an empty bedsit after Grab-a-Granny night at the local disco.

Richard Littlejohn

If you give Congress a dollar of unnecessary taxes, they'll spend about 1.75 dollars and that's inflationary. Inflation is unAmerican, therefore tax avoidance is patriotic.

William Donoghue

The most terrifying words in the English language are, 'I'm from the government and I'm here to help.'

Ronald Reagan

The honourable member for Bourke has committed every crime in the calendar – except the one we could so easily have forgiven him – suicide.

Henry Parkes

I have nothing against Nicholas Ridley's wife or family, but I think it is time he spent more time with them.

Philip Goodhart

I have seen better-looking faces than Alec Douglas-Home's on pirate flags.

John Agar

We've never had a President named Bob. I think it's about time we had one.

Bob Dole

I still play the saxophone because I don't have much job security.

Bill Clinton

A man that would expect to train lobsters to fly in a year is called a lunatic; but a man that thinks men can be turned into angels by an election is a reformer and remains at large.

Finley Peter Dunne

The first mistake in politics is the going into it.

Benjamin Franklin

Prayer never seems to work for me on the golf course. I think this has something to do with my being a terrible putter.

Billy Graham

I often think how much easier the world would have been to manage if Herr Hitler and Signor Mussolini had been to Oxford.

Lord Halifax

Jimmy Hoffa's most valuable contribution to the American labour movement came at the moment he stopped breathing on July 3, 1975.

Dan Moldea

John Major makes George Bush seem like a personality.

Jackie Mason

Democracy is that system of government under which the people having 35,717,342 native-born adult whites to choose from, including thousands who are handsome and many of whom are wise, pick out Coolidge as head of state.

H.L. Mencken

Australian communists are pathological exhibits, human scum, paranoics, degenerates, morons, bludgers, pack of dingoes, industrial outlaws and political lepers, ratbags. If these people went to Russia, Stalin wouldn't even use them for manure.

Arthur Caldwell

Progress in the Foreign Service is either vaginal or rectal. You either marry the boss's daughter or you crawl up his bottom.

Nicholas Monsarrat

I am being frank about myself in this book. I tell of my first mistake on page 850.

Henry Kissinger

Politics

Many MPs never see the London that exists beyond the wine bars and brothels of Westminster.

Ken Livingstone

You can always get the truth from an American statesman after he has turned seventy, or given up all hope of the Presidency.

Wendell Phillips

Public speaking is very easy.

Dan Quayle

It is said that Mr Gladstone could persuade most people of most things, and himself of anything.

W.R. Inge

John Major is the only man who ran away from the circus to become an accountant.

Edward Pearce

Lady Astor told me that if I were her husband, she would put poison in my tea. I retorted by saying that if I were her husband, I would drink it.

Winston Churchill

I want loyalty. I want him to kiss my ass in Macy's window at high noon and tell me it smells like roses.

Lyndon B. Johnson

I seldom think of politics more than eighteen hours a day.
Lyndon B. Johnson

A Conservative is a statesman who is enamored of existing evils, as distinguished from the Liberal, who wishes to replace them with others.
Ambrose Bierce

Spiro Agnew's library burned down and both books were destroyed – and one of them hadn't even been coloured in.
Mort Sahl

There's always room at the top – after the investigation.
Oliver Herford

John Tyler has been called a mediocre man; but this is unwarranted flattery. He was a politician of monumental littleness.
Theodore Roosevelt

I think I can say, and say with pride, that we have some legislatures that bring higher prices than any in the world.
Mark Twain

I am against vice in every form, including the Vice Presidency.
Morris K. Udall

Bill Clinton is the only politician in the world who can distract people's attention from one sex scandal by becoming involved in another.

Matthew Campbell

The biggest danger for a politician is to shake hands with a man who is physically stronger, has been drinking and is voting for the other fellow.

William Proxmire

I stand by all the misstatements I've made.

Dan Quayle

For a working man or woman to vote Republican this year is the same as a chicken voting for Colonel Sanders.

Walter Mondale

The rhinoceros is an animal with a hide two feet thick, and no apparent interest in politics. What a waste.

James Wright

The Democratic Party is like a mule. It has neither pride of ancestry nor hope of posterity.

Ignatius Donnelly

Sales of sleeping pills drop alarmingly during party political broadcasts.

Mitchell Symons

It is not a lie, it's a terminological inexactitude.

Alexander Haig

Asked if they would have sex with President Clinton, 90 per cent of American women replied 'Never again.'

Albert Roge

Edwina Currie has done about as much for the Tory Party as King Herod did for babysitting.

Andrew MacKay

If Jeanne Kirkpatrick were George Bush's running mate, at least there would be some macho on the ticket.

Graham Jones

A zebra cannot change his spots.

Dan Quayle

Bill Clinton operates from the Oral Office in the White House.

Albert Roge

In the House of Commons Peter Snape accused Transport Secretary Nicholas Ridley of being 'a hypocrite' and 'an old Etonian twerp.' He was immediately asked by the speaker to withdraw the word 'hypocrite'.

Graham Jones

Politics

A low voter turnout is an indication that fewer people are going to the polls.

Dan Quayle

Now and then an innocent person is sent to the legislature.

Mark Twain

Receiving support from Ted Heath in a by-election is like being measured by an undertaker.

George Gardiner

John Major collects political jokes – in fact he's got a whole Cabinet full of them.

Graham Jones

If one morning I walked on top of the water across the Potomac River, the headline that afternoon would read PRESIDENT CAN'T SWIM.

Lyndon B. Johnson

The Secret Service have orders to protect Hillary because if she is shot, Bill becomes President.

Bill Casey

I am not politically incorrect. I am just politically challenged.

Matt Bloom

Oswald Moseley was a cross between a demented Terry Thomas and Bill Clinton.

David Aaronovitch

Henry Campbell-Bannerman is remembered chiefly as the man about whom all is forgotten.

Nicholas Bentley

Mr Macmillan is the best Prime Minister we have.

R.A. Butler

Harold Macmillan and I exchanged many frank words in our respective languages.

Peter Cook

Religion

✝ Religion

I've always fancied being a monk – drinking mead, tending gardens and making honey.

Vic Reeves

If there is no Hell, a good many preachers are obtaining money under false pretences.

William Sunday

More people are driven insane through religious hysteria than by drinking alcohol.

W.C. Fields

I admire the Pope. I have a lot of respect for anyone who can tour without an album.

Rita Rudner

In the beginning there was nothing and God said 'Let there be light', and there was still nothing, but everybody could see it.

Dave Thomas

Those characters in the Bible who rent their garments – wouldn't it have been less expensive to buy them in the first place?

Paul Merton

The good Lord never gives you more than you can handle. Unless you die of something.

Steve Martin

I am half-Catholic and half-Jewish. When I go to confession, I bring my lawyer with me.

Ed Mann

One half of the world does not believe in God and the other half does not believe in me.

Oscar Wilde

He stopped sinning suddenly – he died.

Elbert Hubbard

So my dear brethren which would you prefer, to be in the light with the five wise virgins or in the dark with the five foolish virgins?

Alan Bennett

Being a Catholic doesn't stop you from sinning. It just stops you from enjoying it.

Cleveland Amory

In some copies of the article 'The Power of the Papacy' the Pope was described as His Satanic Majesty. This should have read The Roman Antichrist.

Ian Paisley

Sailors ought never to go to church. They ought to go to hell, where it is much more comfortable.

H. G. Wells

✝ Religion

I don't think God gets enough recognition for what He does.

Mandy Smith

I do not accept the word of the slanderous bachelor who lives on the banks of the Tiber.

Ian Paisley

The merit claimed for the Anglican Church is that, if you let it alone, it will let you alone.

Ralph W. Emerson

If absolute power corrupts absolutely, where does that leave God?

George Deacon

I have four children, which is not bad considering I am not a Catholic.

Peter Ustinov

God in his goodness gave us brains so that we would have the wisdom to know when not to use them.

Hugh Leonard

There can hardly be a town in the South of England where you could throw a brick without hitting the niece of a bishop.

George Orwell

I never pray on a golf course. Actually, the Lord answers my prayers everywhere except on the course.

Bill Graham

The one thing father always gave up for Lent was going to church.

Clarence Day

Merit, indeed! We are come to a pretty pass if they talk of merit for a bishopric.

Lord Westmorland

Almost all religions agree that God is fond of music, sometimes of dancing and always of processions.

Robert Morley

As the poet said, 'Only God can make a tree,' probably because it's so hard to figure out how to get the bark on.

Woody Allen

I dislike blasphemy on purely rational grounds. If there is no God, blasphemy is stupid and unnecessary; if there is, it's damned dangerous.

Flann O'Brien

Florence Nightingale felt towards God as she might have felt towards a glorified sanitary engineer; and in some of her speculations she seems hardly to distinguish between the Deity and the Drains.

Lytton Strachey

✝ Religion

The day the Catholic and Protestant churches combine, it's the end of all drinking. I'll have to go to Rome to sabotage the affair.

Brendan Behan

The primary function of a priest is to keep his congregation awake.

Peter Ustinov

My friends in Christian Coalition, no matter how rough the road may be, we can and we will, never, never surrender to what is right.

Dan Quayle

If God had intended us to fly, he would have made it easier to get to the airport.

Jonathan Winters

And God said, 'Let there be light'; and there was light, but the Electricity Board said He would have to wait until Thursday to be connected. And God saw the light and it was good; He saw the quarterly bill and that was not good.

Spike Milligan

The Book of Mormon is chloroform in print.

Mark Twain

If ever I come face to face with my maker, I shall say 'God, why did you make the evidence for your existence so insufficient?'

Bertrand Russell

Religion

I read the Book of Job last night – I don't think God comes well out of it.

Virginia Woolf

I hear Glenn Hoddle has found God. That must have been one hell of a pass.

Bob Davies

One goldfish told another that he intended to become an atheist. 'Don't be crazy,' the other goldfish replied, 'of course there's a God – who do you think changes the water every day?'

Richard Needham

Eternal nothingness is fine if you happen to be dressed for it.

Woody Allen

At the moment I'm working on a non-fiction version of the Warren Report.

Woody Allen

In 1969 I published a small book on Humility. It was a pioneering work which has not, to my knowledge, been surperseded.

Frank Longford

I shall walk, nay I shall run, through the Valley of Death.

Woody Allen

A survey revealed that 96 per cent of Americans believe in God, 90 per cent pray regularly, 71 per cent believe in an afterlife, and 41 per cent attend church once a week. Another poll found that 3 per cent believe they are God.

James Adams

The Lord created the universe in seven days but the Lord had the wonderful advantage of being able to work alone.

Kofi Annan

The average minister should be unfrocked immediately and prevented, by force if necessary, from communicating any ideas to persons under thirty-five.

W.C. Fields

A sixty-two-year-old friend of mine went to bed at night and prayed, 'Please God give me skin like a teenager's'. Next day, she woke up with acne.

Phyllis Diller

If you're going to sin, sin against God, not the bureaucracy. God will forgive you but the bureaucracy won't.

Hyman Rickover

An Anglican clergyman is invisible six days a week and incomprehensible on the seventh.

Dean Inge

On one occasion when the Reverend Laurence Chaderton had been preaching for over two hours, he is said to have shown signs of flagging. The congregation then cried out, with one voice: 'For God's sake, Sir, go on!'

Henry Button

Walking in a churchyard I have often asked myself, 'Where are all the bad people buried?'

Charles Lamb

Between projects, I go into the park and bite the grass and wail, 'Why do You make me aware of the fact that I have to die one day?' God says, 'Please, I have Chinese people yelling at me, I haven't time for this.' I say all right. God is like a Jewish waiter, he has too many tables.

Mel Brooks

No mention of God. They keep him up their sleeve for as long as they can, vicars do. They know it puts people off.

Alan Bennett

Methodism is not really a religion – it's just a sort of insurance policy in case there does turn out to be a God.

Peter Barr

Most of your parishioners will meet you on only three occasions. The first and last, baptism and burial, they are not conscious at all. And the middle one, holy matrimony, they are barely half conscious, if that.

Kenneth Haworth

✝ Religion

As luck would have it, Providence was on my side.

Samuel Butler

She believed in nothing. Only her scepticism kept her from being an atheist.

Jean-Paul Sartre

Woody Allen has a face that convinces you that God is a cartoonist.

Jack Kroll

I have always been amazed that women are allowed to enter churches. What sort of conversations can they have with God?

Charles Baudelaire

Every human being commits 630,720,000 sins by the age of thirty.

Augustus Toplady

There is not the least use in preaching to anyone unless you chance to catch them ill.

Sydney Smith

Lest O Lord this prayer be too obscure, permit thy servant to illustrate it with an anecdote.

Allan Laing

I dreamt last night I was in hell: It was just like a missionary meeting – I couldn't get near the fire for parsons.

Samuel Wilberforce

Satan, who has during all time maintained the imposing position of spiritual head of four-fifths of the human race and political head of the whole of it, must be granted the possession of executive abilities of the loftiest order.

Mark Twain

If it turns out that there is a God, I don't think that he's evil. But the worst you can say about him is that he's an underachiever.

Woody Allen

What a pity that Noah and his party didn't miss the boat.

Mark Twain

I have a fear that there is an afterlife but no one will know where it's being held.

Woody Allen

There are three sorts of country parson in my diocese. Those who have gone out of their minds. Those who are going out of their minds. And those who have no minds to go out of.

Edward King

To you I'm an atheist; to God, I'm the loyal opposition.

Woody Allen

✝ Religion

If God can do anything, can He make a stone so heavy that He cannot lift it?

A.A. Milne

His was the sort of career that made the Recording Angel think seriously about taking up shorthand.

Nicholas Bentley

In the beginning, the universe was created. This has made a lot of people very angry, and is generally considered to be have been a bad move.

Douglas Adams

The Bible doesn't forbid suicide. It's a Catholic directive, intended to slow down their loss of martyrs.

Ellen Blackstone

I'd love to see Christ come back to crush the spirit of hate and make men put down their guns. I'd also like just one more hit single.

Tiny Tim

Giving away a fortune is carrying Christianity too far.

Charlotte Bingham

Serving God is doing good to man, but praying is thought an easier service and therefore more generally chosen.

Benjamin Franklin

It is the function of vice to keep virtue within reasonable bounds.

Samuel Butler

I'm going to take a moment to contemplate most of the Western religions. I'm looking for something soft on morality, generous with holidays, and with a very short initiation period.

David Addison

Mohammed is one of the most common Christian names in the world.

David Jensen

I know God will not give me anything I can't handle. I just wish that He didn't trust me so much.

Mother Teresa

I once asked a man what he thought would happen to him after he died. He replied that he believed he would inherit eternal bliss, but he didn't wish to talk about such unpleasant subjects.

F.W. Myers

A lie is a very poor substitute for the truth, but the only one known to date.

Ambrose Bierce

Lutherans are like Scottish people, only with less frivolity.

Garrison Keillor

Religion

Only a vegan nun who has taken a vow of silence lives
without hurting anyone.

Tim Rayment

Of course heaven forbids certain pleasures, but one finds
means of compromise.

Molière

There is a charm about the forbidden that makes it
unspeakably desirable.

Mark Twain

Everybody has a God-given right to be an atheist.

Michael Patton

December 10, 1777 Jas. Soaper hanged for stealing a nail.
December 14, 1777 Jas. Soaper found to be innocent.
December 17, 1777 Jas. Soaper dug up and removed to
Consecrated Ground.

Michael Green

Science and Technology

To protect yourself from nuclear radiation, all you have to do is to go down to the bottom of your swimming pool and hold your breath.

David Miller

I am an expert on electricity. My father occupied the chair of applied electricity at the State Prison.

W.C. Fields

Weather forecast for tonight: dark.

George Carlin

What is algebra exactly? Is it those three-cornered things?

J.M. Barrie

Quod Erat Demonstrandum is Latin for 'Don't argue with ME, you bastard.'

Russell Bell

The heart of the airport security system is the metal detector, a device that shoots invisible rays into your body. According to security personnel, these rays are perfectly harmless, although you notice that THEY never go through the metal detector. In fact, when nobody's around, they use it to cook their lunch.

Dave Barry

Science and Technology

I saw Cher on TV promoting a sugar substitute. She said,
'You care more about what you put in your car than you do
about what you put in your body.' Thanks, Cher. But I never
put silicone breast implants in my car.

Denis Leary

The trouble with the Internet is that it is replacing
masturbation as a leisure activity.

Patrick Murray

If the B-2 is invisible, why don't we just announce we've
built a hundred of them and not build them?

John Kasich

The Irish Sea is naturally radioactive. The Sellafield
discharges are less radioactive than the sea they are
discharged into.

Cecil Parkinson

A tree is a tree. How many more do you need to look at?

Ronald Reagan

The most dreaded words in the English language are 'some
assembly required'.

Bill Cosby

Electricity is of two kinds, positive and negative. The
difference is, I presume, that one comes a little more
expensive, but is more durable; the other is a cheaper thing,
but the moths get into it.

Stephen Leacock

You ask me if I keep a notebook in which to record my great ideas. I've only ever had one.

Albert Einstein

Beware of experts. The day humans blow up the world with The Bomb the last survivor will be an expert saying it can never happen.

Peter Ustinov

The best thing about the rain forests is that they never suffer from drought.

Dan Quayle

A Danish lady of one hundred and four was summoned to enrol in a nursery school because the computer only went up to ninety-nine and she appeared on the records as being five years old.

Peter Ustinov

You can stop almost anything from functioning by hitting it with a large rock.

Russell Bell

Well, if I called the wrong number, why did you answer the phone?

James Thurber

A stitch in time would have confused Einstein.

Steven Wright

Ghosts can walk through walls, how come they don't fall through the floor?

Steven Wright

Fish are so underrated these days, especially sand dabs – all of them really. I could go on and on about it. I do, actually. People say to me, 'Don't go on about fish today, please, Jack'. And I say, 'Just tell me one thing – can you breathe under water?' And of course, I have them there.

John Cleese

A bishop wrote gravely to the *Times* inviting all nations to destroy 'the formula' of the atomic bomb. There is no simple remedy for ignorance so abysmal.

Peter Medaway

The wise individual doesn't get too attached to any of life's pleasures, knowing that wonderful science is hard at work proving it's bad for him.

Bill Vaughan

If builders built buildings the way computer programmers write programs, the first woodpecker that came along would destroy civilisation.

Reede Stockton

The only reason we had a son was to get someone to work the video. For ten years we used it as a night light.

Adrian Walsh

Science and Technology

The ancient Greeks, aided by a warm climate invented geometry and they used this advanced knowledge to conquer the surrounding cultures by piercing them with the ends of isosceles triangles.

Dave Barry

Everything that can be invented has been invented.

Charles Duell

Sponges grow in the ocean. That kills me. I wonder how much deeper the ocean would be if that didn't happen?

Steven Wright

The greatest unsolved problem in science is this – how can you be sitting on a damp towel for half an hour and not realise it until you stand up?

Patrick Murray

Automatic simply means that you cannot repair it yourself.

Frank Capra

I am convinced UFOs exist because I have seen one.

Jimmy Carter

It is to be regretted that domestication has seriously deteriorated the moral character of the duck. In the wild state he is a faithful husband; but no sooner is he domesticated than he becomes polygamous, and makes nothing of owning ten or a dozen wives at a time.

Isabella Beaton

Mathematics was always my bad subject. I couldn't convince my teachers that many of my answers were meant ironically.

Calvin Trillin

Why is it that everything else can be written on paper, but mathematics and cave paintings have to be done in chalk?

A.A. Gill

Eighty-two point six per cent of statistics are made up on the spot.

Vic Reeves

Have you ever smelt a rain forest? They stink. They stink worse than a 13-year-old's bedroom.

A.A. Gill

An expert is a man who has stopped thinking. Why should he think? He is an expert!

Frank Lloyd Wright

The New York State Museum found my wife's shoe. On the basis of its measurements, they constructed a dinosaur.

Woody Allen

Life is anything that dies when you stamp on it.

Dave Barry

Beware of computer programmers who carry screwdrivers.

Leonard Brandwein

UNIX is basically a simple operating system, but you have to be a genius to understand the simplicity.

Dennis Ritchie

The factory of the future will have only two employees, a man and a dog. The man will be there to feed the dog. The dog will there to keep the man from touching the equipment.

Warren G. Bennis

If rhino horn is such a powerful aphrodisiac, why are rhinos an endangered species?

Rory McGrath

The best defence against the atom bomb is not to be there when it goes off.

Winston Churchill

Printing broke out in the province of Kansu in AD 86. The early Chinese simply could not let well enough alone.

Bill Cuppy

The secret of creativity is knowing how to hide your sources.

Albert Einstein

The perfect computer has been developed. You just feed in your problems and they never come out again.

Al Goodman

The greatest invention in history is the safety pin. The second greatest is perforated toilet paper.

Tiny Tim

Death is a low chemical trick played on everybody except sequoia trees.

J.J. Furnas

He has an IQ of about room temperature.

Dan Hampton

The avocado is a lavatory-coloured fruit.

Mike Barfield

The Fourth Law of Thermodynamics states that if the probability of success is not almost one, then it is damn near zero.

David Ellis

Recent evidence suggests that normal body temperature is 89.4°F and that mankind is running a temperature.

Cully Abrell

Many snakes are actually quite short if you don't count the tail.

John Thompson

Monkeys and apes have the ability to speak but keep silent to avoid being put to work.

René Descartes

Science and Technology

In France in the eighteenth century a combination lock was exhibited which required 3,674,385 turns of the dial to open and close it. It took one man 120 nights to lock and another man an additional 120 nights to unlock.

Bruce Felton

If everyone on earth stopped breathing for just an hour, the greenhouse effect would no longer be a problem.

Jerry Adler

Jocky Wilson is the minimum of mass into which a human being can be contracted.

Nancy Banks-Smith

The ant sets an example to us all, but it is not a good one.

Max Beerbohm

An old lady of my acquaintance went into her greengrocer's and asked for a pound of potatoes. On being told that everything was kilos now, she said, 'All right, I'll have a pound of kilos then.'

Matthew Parris

Virtual reality is a cutting edge computer science project in which companies are investing millions of dollars in a frenzied attempt to reproduce an effect which can currently be achieved by simply looking out of the window.

Mike Barfield

My dog understands every word I say but ignores it.

Michael Green

The smallest hole will eventually empty the largest container, unless it is made intentionally for drainage, in which case it will clog.

Dave Grissom

The most overlooked advantage to owning a computer is that if they foul up there's no law against whacking them around a little.

Eric Porterfield

Chaos Theory is a new theory invented by scientists panicked by the thought that the public were beginning to understand the old ones.

Mike Barfield

Scientists have discovered a noise made just prior to the Big Bang which sounds something like 'oops'.

Cully Abrell

Sex is just the mathematics urge sublimated.

M.C. Reed

He was a multi-millionaire. He made all his money designing the little diagrams that tell which way to put batteries in.

Steven Wright

Science and Technology

In Vegas I got into a long argument with the man at the roulette wheel over what I considered to be an odd number.

Steven Wright

If ants are such busy workers, how come they find time to go to all the picnics?

Marie Dressler

The best way to tell gold is to pass a nugget around in a crowded bar. if it comes back, it's not gold.

Lennie Lower

Social Behaviour and Manners

These are my principles. If you don't like them I have others.

Groucho Marx

I always take a nap before I go to bed.

W.C. Fields

I must particularly warn you against laughing; and I could heartily wish that you may be often seen to smile, but never heard to laugh. Frequent and loud laughter is the characteristic of folly and ill manners: it is the manner in which the mob express their silly joy at silly things. To my mind there is nothing so illiberal, and so ill-bred, as audible laughter.

Lord Chesterfield

It always rains on tents. Rainstorms will travel thousands of miles against the prevailing winds for the opportunity to rain on a tent.

Dave Barry

My only solution for the problem of habitual accidents is to stay in bed all day. Even then, there is always the chance that you will fall out.

Robert Benchley

We kept trying to set up a small anarchist community, but people wouldn't obey the rules.

Alan Bennett

I never accepted a knighthood because to be me is honour enough. Besides, they get one into disreputable company.

George Bernard Shaw

One should never put on one's best trousers to go out to battle for freedom and truth.

Henryk Ibsen

If you have anything of importance to tell me, for God's sake begin at the end.

Sara Duncan

Whether it is summer or winter, I always like to have the morning well aired before I get up.

Beau Brummell

In life it is difficult to say who does you the most mischief, enemies with the worst intentions or friends with the best.

Edward Bulwer-Lytton

In a civil war a general must know exactly when to move over to the other side.

Henry Reed

She had lost the art of conversation, but not, unfortunately, the power of speech.

George Bernard Shaw

If you can't laugh at yourself, make fun of other people.

Bobby Slayton

There are now groups of grown men going on self-discovery weekends, marching into the mountains, joining hands in moonlit forests, howling and beating drums. They pay money to do this. Personally, I like to do the same thing in my living room while I'm watching the Super Bowl. But I do it alone.

Denis Leary

Impotence and sodomy are socially OK but birth control is flagrantly middle class.

Evelyn Waugh

The nice thing about being a celebrity is that if you bore people they think it's their fault.

Henry Kissinger

Camping is nature's way of promoting the motel industry.

Dave Barry

To ask the Queen for a cigarette is rock bottom.

Jeffrey Bernard

Creep up behind a nightclub bouncer and hit him over the head with a wet fish. What follows is an example of 'response to stimuli' as well as a sojourn in the intensive care unit of your choice.

Russell Bell

The cocktail party is a device for paying off obligations to people you don't want to invite to dinner.

Charles Smith

Being a star has made it possible for me to get insulted in places where the average negro could never hope to go and get insulted.

Sammy Davis Jr

There is no stronger craving in the world than that of the rich for titles, except perhaps that of the titled for riches.

Hesketh Pearson

I was in a beauty contest once. I not only came in last, I was hit in the mouth by Miss Congeniality.

Phyllis Diller

I was driving down the highway, saw a sign that said 'Next Rest Area 25 miles'! I said, 'Wow, that's pretty big. People must get really tired around here.'

Steven Wright

He was the sort of fellow that would insist on being seated in the no-smoking compartment of the lifeboat.

John Pepper

Cockroaches and socialites are the only things that can stay up all night and eat anything.

Herb Caen

O wad some power the giftie gie us to see some people before they see us.

Ethel W. Mumford

I am firm; you are obstinate; he is a pig-headed fool.

Bertrand Russell

If you're going to do something tonight that you'll be sorry for tomorrow morning, sleep late.

Henny Youngman

To be positive is to be mistaken at the top of one's voice.

Ambrose Bierce

Never call a man a fool. Borrow from him.

W.C. Fields

I do not have to forgive my enemies, I have had them all shot.

Ramon Narvalez

One never trusts anyone that one has deceived.

Oscar Wilde

Clothes make the man. Naked people have little or no influence on society.

Mark Twain

Most of the time I don't have much fun. The rest of the time I don't have any fun at all.

Woody Allen

Nothing beats blackmail at securing absolute allegiance.

M.A. Sharp

Every day my grandfather made us stand in a little room together, side by side, looking straight ahead for three minutes without talking to each other. He told me it was elevator practice.

Steven Wright

Fashion is what one wears oneself.

Oscar Wilde

There's a name for you ladies, but it's not used in high society outside of kennels.

W.C. Fields

In Australia I had a long talk with the Governor's wife. We talked about the mating habits of the wallaby.

W.C. Fields

A man who is angry on the right grounds and with the right people, and in the right manner and at the right moment for the right length of time, is to be praised.

Aristotle

A friend that ain't in need is a friend indeed.

Kin Hubbard

The urge to gamble is so universal and its practice so pleasurable that I assume it must be evil.

Heywood Broun

Hermits have no peer pressure.

Steven Wright

A well tied tie is the first serious step in life.

Oscar Wilde

My favourite chair is a wicker chair. It's my favourite chair because I stole it. I was at a party, a very crowded party, and when no one was looking I went over to it and I unravelled it and stuck it through the keyhole in the door. The girl who was in it was almost killed.

Steven Wright

A friend in need is a pest – get rid of him.

Tommy Cooper

I was sitting in a restaurant the other day and there's a bloke sitting next to me with a really stupid haircut, so I hit him. Nobody takes the piss out of me.

Paul Merton

Speak softly and carry a big carrot.

Howard Laver

Very sorry I can't come. Lie follows by post.

Charles Beresford

The hardest thing in the world to stop is a temporary chairman.

Kin Hubbard

Dear Randolph Churchill – quite unspoiled by failure.

Noel Coward

Honesty is a good thing but it is not profitable to its possessor unless it is kept under control.

Don Marquis

Each of us as he receives his private trouncings at the hands of fate is kept in good heart by the moth in his brother's parachute, and the scorpion in his neighbour's underwear.

N.F. Simpson

If a woman likes another woman, she's cordial. If she doesn't like her, she's very cordial.

Irvin S. Cobb

I believe in the discipline of silence and could talk for hours about it.

George Bernard Shaw

The only way to atone for being a little over-dressed is by being always absolutely over-educated.

Oscar Wilde

Just when you're beginning to think pretty well of people, you run across somebody who puts sugar on sliced tomatoes.

Will Cuppy

We invite people like Betjeman to tea, but we don't marry
them.

Lady Chetwode

I'm not superstitious. I'm afraid it would bring me bad luck.

Babe Ruth

Egotism is the anaesthetic that dulls the pain of stupidity.

Frank Leahy

And when they were up they were up,
And when they were down they were down,
And when they were only halfway up, I was arrested.

Spike Milligan

People are much more willing to lend you books than
bookcases.

Mark Twain

A depressed person is someone who, if he is in the bath, will
not get out to answer the telephone.

Questin Crisp

His huff arrived, and he departed in it.

Alexander Woollcott

Love your enemies, just in case your friends turn out to be a
bunch of bastards.

R.A. Dickson

People who live in glass houses have to answer the bell.

Bruce Patterson

Of course I wouldn't say anything about her unless I could say something good. And, oh boy is this good.

Bill King

Why doesn't everybody leave everybody else the hell alone?

Jimmy Durante

My principal pastime is the daily avoidance of assorted professional beggars, alcoholics and deranged individuals.

George Salmond

There are no more liberals – they've all been mugged.

James Wilson

Philanthropy is the refuge of people who wish to annoy their fellow creatures.

Oscar Wilde

Nothing needs reforming so much as other people's habits.

Mark Twain

You probably wouldn't worry about what people think of you if you could know how seldom they do.

Olin Miller

Whenever people talk to me about the weather, I always feel certain that they mean something else.

Oscar Wilde

The secret of making oneself tiresome is not to know when to stop.

Voltaire

To be an ideal guest, stay at home.

E. W. Howe

If someone tells you he is going to make a 'realistic decision', you immediately understand that he has resolved to do something bad.

Mary McCarthy

We shall always keep a spare corner in our heads to give passing hospitality to our friends' opinions.

Joseph Joubert

When a fellow says, 'Well, to make a long story short,' it's too late.

Don Herold

Some people never use their initiative because nobody ever tells them to.

Mike Smith

My favourite way of wasting time is trying to say something in praise of paper towels.

Franklin P. Adams

There was laughter in the back of the theatre, leading to the belief that somebody was telling jokes back there.

George S. Kaufman

Other people are quite dreadful. The only possible society is oneself.

Oscar Wilde

The greatest happiness is to scatter your enemy, to drive him before you, to see his cities reduced to ashes, to see those who love him shrouded in tears, and to gather into your bosom his wives and daughters.

Genghis Khan

The little trouble in the world that is not due to love is due to friendship.

E. W. Howe

I have been complimented many times and they always embarrass me; I always feel that they have not said enough.

Mark Twain

Sport

Sure, luck means a lot in football. Not having a good quarterback is bad luck.

Don Schula

Any time Detroit scores more than 100 points and holds the other team below 100 points they almost always win.

Doug Collins

My wins are merely beginner's luck, gentlemen, although I have devoted some time to the game.

W.C. Fields

Someone threw a petrol bomb at Alex Higgins once and he drank it.

Frank Carson

There comes a time in every man's life and I've had plenty of them.

Casey Stengel

Nobody has ever bet enough on a winning horse.

Richard Sasuly

The news of the Pope's death puts a damper even on a Yankee win.

Phil Rizzuto

More lampshades were broken in Britain by golf clubs than by Hitler's bombers.

Val Doonican

In 1971 I was sent off the field for arguing with one of my own team-mates.

George Best

Sure there have been deaths and injuries in boxing, but none of them serious.

Alan Winter

I once got a ball out of a St Andrews bunker in two. I'm not saying God couldn't have got it out in one, but He would have had to throw it.

Arnold Palmer

Ninety-five per cent of putts which finish short don't go in.

Hubert Green

However unlucky you may be on the golf course it really is not fair to expect your adversary's grief for your undeserved misfortunes to be as poignant as your own.

Horace Hutchinson

Golf architects can't play golf themselves and make damn sure that no one else can.

Lee Trevino

These greens are so fast I have to hold my putter over the ball and hit it with the shadow.

Sam Snead

 **Sport**

When golf first started, one under par was a birdie, two under par was an eagle and three under par was a partridge. They had to change that because you couldn't get a partridge on a par three.

John MacKay

It may have been the greatest four-wood anyone ever hit. It was so much on the flag that I had to lean sideways to follow the flight of the ball.

Gary Player

I was watching what I thought was sumo wrestling on the television for two hours before I realised it was darts.

Hattie Hayridge

I can never figure out what would make ten thousand people run twenty-six miles. Maybe there's a Hare Krishna behind them going, 'Excuse me, can I talk to you for just a second?'

Rita Rudner

Show me a man who is a good loser, and I'll show you a man who is playing golf with his boss.

Jim Murray

You can talk to a fade but a hook won't listen.

Lee Trevino

I owe everything to golf. Where else would a guy with an IQ like mine earn so much money?

Hubert Green

Pavarotti is very difficult to pass at the net in tennis with or without a racquet.

Peter Ustinov

Is my friend in the bunker or is the bastard on the green?

David Feherty

I was asked to be a linesman at the Wimbledon tennis championship. I excused myself by expressing myself flattered by the offer, but begged them to renew it when my eyesight had deteriorated sufficiently to be able to make wrong decisions with absolute conviction.

Peter Ustinov

A golfer needs a loving wife to whom he can describe the day's play through the long evening.

P.G. Wodehouse

In my singles match I saw Hope vanishing over the horizon with her arse on fire.

David Feherty

Never break your putter and your driver in the same round or you're dead.

Tommy Bolt

In the USA first-class golfers take as long to choose a wife as a club. Sometimes they make the wrong choice in each case.

Dai Rees

Sport

Proficiency at billiards is a sign of a misspent youth.

Samuel Johnson

If women were meant to play football, God would have put their tits somewhere else.

Gordon Sinclair

I have told the team that if we don't give away a goal, we don't lose.

Terry Venables

You can't lose an old golf ball.

John Willis

The other lads on the rugby team are calling me 'Lurpak' – the best butter in the world.

Steve Hampson

Golf and sex are about the only things you can enjoy without being good at it.

Jimmy Demaret

The fairway is a narrow strip of mown grass that separates two groups of golfers looking for lost balls in the rough.

Henry Beard

I've just had a hole-in-one at the sixteenth and I left the ball in the hole just to prove it.

Bob Hope

A goalkeeper is a goalkeeper because he can't play football.

Ruud Gullit

If your caddie says to you on the tee, 'Hit it down the left side with a little draw,' ignore him. All you do on the tee is try not to hit the caddie.

Jim Murray

Once rugby players have succeeded in getting their boots on the right feet, the mental challenge of the game is largely over.

Derek Robinson

It is now known that Darwin was a golfer – he set out in search of the missing links.

Sam Gross

Give me a millionaire with a bad back swing, and I can have a very pleasant afternoon.

George Law

If your adversary is badly bunkered, there is no rule against your standing over him and counting his strokes aloud, with increasing gusto as their number mounts up; but it will be a wise precaution to arm yourself with the niblick before doing so, so as to meet him on equal terms.

Horace Hutchinson

The word 'aerobics' came about when the gym instructors got together and said 'If we're going to charge ten dollars an hour, we can't call it 'jumping up and down'.

Rita Rudner

I can't cheat on my score – all you have to do is to look back down the fairway and count the wounded.

Bob Hope

If one synchronised swimmer drowns, do all the rest have to drown too?

Wright Stevens

Real golfers go to work to relax.

George Dillon

You don't have to be certifiably insane to be a jump jockey but it does give you the edge over the competition.

Graham Sharpe

Dear Lord, if there is cricket in heaven, let there also be rain.

Alec Douglas-Home

Hagen said that no one remembers who finished second. But they still ask me if I ever think about that putt I missed to win the 1970 Open at St Andrews. I tell them that sometimes it doesn't cross my mind for a full five minutes.

Doug Saunders

People will think I'm crackers taking over at Birmingham City. I'm voluntarily going back into the madhouse.

Trevor Francis

A professional will tell you the amount of flex you need in the shaft of your club. The more the flex, the more strength you will need to break the thing over your knees.

Stephen Baker

I am a jockey because I was too small to be a window cleaner and too big to be a garden gnome.

Adrian Maguire

A Coarse Golfer is one who has to shout 'Fore' when he putts.

Michael Green

No horse can go as fast as the money you put on it.

Earl Wilson

My favourite shots in golf are the practice swing and the conceded putt. The rest can never be mastered.

Lord Robertson

Most people play a fair game of golf – if you watch them.

Joey Adams

At Glasgow Rangers I was third choice left-back behind an amputee and a Catholic.

Craig Brown

A hole-in-one is an occurrence in which a ball is hit directly from the tee into the hole on a single shot by a golfer playing alone.

Roy McKie

I don't follow particular horses, although horses I back seem to.

Tommy Docherty

My trouble on the golf course is that I stand too close to my shots after I've hit them.

Bob Hope

If Ben Hogan means to win, you lose.

Henry Longhurst

Golf is a game in which you yell 'fore', shoot six and put down five.

Paul Harvey

An ante-post bet is simply a way of prolonging life. A man holding an ante-post voucher never dies before the race itself is over.

Jeffrey Bernard

Secretariat is everything I am not. He's young, he's beautiful, he has lots of hair, he's fast, he's durable, he has a large bank account, and his entire sex life is ahead of him.

Si Burick

If you're playing a poker game and you look round the table and you can't tell who the sucker is, it's you.

Paul Newman

I used to play golf with a guy who cheated so badly that he had a hole-in-one and wrote down zero on his scorecard.

Bob Bruce

Paul Kelleway would fancy his chances on a pregnant rhinoceros.

Nick Green

After shooting over 200 I asked my partner what I should give the caddie. He replied, 'Your golf clubs'.

Jackie Gleason

I was summoned to appear before the golf club committee for playing off the ladies' tee. I explained I was playing my third shot.

Bing Crosby

Golf is a game in which a sphere 1.68" in diameter is placed on a sphere 8,000 miles in diameter. The object is to hit the little sphere, not the big one.

Winston Churchill

If I had my way, any man guilty of golf would be ineligible for any office of trust in the United States.

H.L. Mencken

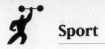

I'm hitting the woods just great, but I'm having a terrible time hitting out of them.

Harry Toscano

I've had more clubs than Nick Faldo.

Tommy Docherty

Any jockey can win on a great horse, but it takes a good jockey to lose on it.

Ernest Hemingway

Be funny on the golf course? Do I kid my best friend's mother about her heart condition?

Phil Silvers

Horse sense is something a horse has that prevents him betting on people.

Father Mathew

Any man who has to save up to go racing has no right to be on a racecourse.

Jeffrey Bernard

Local rules are a set of regulations that are ignored only by players on one specific course rather than by golfers as a whole.

Henry Beard

Playing golf with the President is handy. If you hit a ball into the rough and it drops near a tree, the tree becomes a Secret Service man and moves away.

Bob Hope

Give me a man with big hands, big feet and no brains and I will make a golfer out of him.

Walter Hagen

A man's gotta make at least one bet every day otherwise he could be walking around lucky and never know it.

Jimmy Jones

In the crowd I play with I find it more profitable to keep my eye on my partner than to keep my eye on the ball.

Jim Murray

The secret of missing a tree is to aim straight at it.

Michael Green

When I dislocated my shoulder the nurse said it was a lot less painful than having a baby. I said, 'Let's see what happens if you try to put it back again.'

Stuart Turner

Jack Nicklaus plays a kind of golf with which I am not familiar.

Bobby Jones

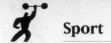

Sport

We can beat anyone on our day so long as we score.

Alex Toten

Daddy, why mustn't the ball go into the little hole?

Herbert V. Prochnow

Paul Gascoigne was waddling around the pitch like a recently impregnated hippopotamus.

Marcus Berkmann

The least thing upset him on the links. He missed short putts because of the uproar of the butterflies in the adjoining meadows.

P. G. Wodehouse

If you want to take long walks, take long walks. If you want to hit things with a stick, hit things with a stick. But there's no excuse for combining the two and putting the results on TV. Golf is not so much a sport as an insult to lawns.

Dave Barry

I once 'skied' a ball so high I had to shout, 'Don't touch it Lord, there's a two-stroke penalty if you do'.

Lee Trevino

Some male athletes have breasts I've only dreamed about.

Ruby Wax

There's a fine line between fishing and just standing on the shore like an idiot.

Steven Wright

The secret of football is to equalise before the opposition scores.

Danny Blanchflower

The invention of the ball was one of the worst tragedies ever to befall mankind and to force small boys on to soggy playing fields every afternoon to kick or throw or hurl these objects at each other for a couple of hours before returning the ball to precisely where they had first found it, is a near criminal waste of time, energy and childhood.

Robert Morley

In baseball I see no reason why the infield should not try to put the batter off his stride at the critical moment, by neatly timed disparagements of his wife's fidelity and his mother's respectability.

George Bernard Shaw

They call it golf because all the other four-letter words were taken.

Walter Hagen

In Russia, if a male athlete loses he becomes a female athlete.

Yakov Smirnoff

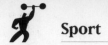

Tony Cascarino is the biggest waste of money since Madonna's father bought her pyjamas.

Frank Lauder

Anybody who finds it easy to make money on the horses is probably in the dog food business.

Franklin P. Jones

Michael Chang has all the fire and passion of a public service announcement, so much so that he makes Pete Sampras appear fascinating.

Alex Ramsay

If you want to know what you'll look like in ten years, look in the mirror after you've run a marathon.

Jeff Scaff

I was swinging like a toilet door on a prawn trawler.

David Feherty

I'm not saying my game is bad at the moment, but if I grew tomatoes, they'd come up sliced.

Lee Trevino

If you hit a pony over the nose at the outset of your acquaintance, he may not love you but he will take a deep interest in your movements ever afterwards.

Rudyard Kipling

Jack Nicklaus isn't really a great golfer. He's just been on a thirty-year lucky streak.

Henry Beard

I'm not happy with our tackling. We're hurting them, but they keep getting up.

Jimmy Murphy

The cocktail party – as the name itself indicates was originally invented by dogs. They are simply bottom sniffings raised to the rank of formal ceremonies.

Lawrence Durrell

Burrough Hill Lad has had more operations than Joan Collins – and maybe more men working on him.

Jenny Pitman

When the force is with Devon Malcolm and he puts his contact lenses in the correct eyes, he can be devastating.

Mike Selvey

One way to stop a runaway horse is to bet on him.

Jeffrey Bernard

It is extremely cold here. The English fielders are keeping their hands in their pockets between balls.

Christopher Martin-Jenkin

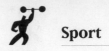 **Sport**

A loving wife is better than making 50 at cricket or even 99; beyond that I will not go.

James Barrie

He hit an opponent around the head with his stick during a polo match. In a sport rooted in protocol both on and off the pitch, there is only one more serious crime – abuse of a pony.

Lin Jenkins

Cricket is the only game that you can actually put on weight when playing.

Tommy Docherty

Golf balls are attracted to water as unerringly as the eye of a middle-aged man to a female bosom.

Michael Green

I take my new football recruits into the woods and start them running. Those that run around the trees are chosen as guards; those that run into the trees are chosen as tackles.

Vince Lombardi

Mickey Mantle can hit them with the left and the right. He's completely amphibious.

Yogi Berra

When you are putting well, you are a good putter; when your opponent is putting well, he has a good putter.

John D. Sheridan

Ted Dexter was a master of placing both feet in his mouth at the same time.

Ian Botham

If in the paddock the owner is surrounded by a herd of young children, don't back his horse. But if the owner is accompanied by a beautiful lady, plunge to the hilt.

Robert Morley

A coarse golfer is one who normally goes from tee to green without touching the fairway.

Michael Green

The secret of playing cricket is to put bat to ball.

W.G. Grace

The real beauty about having Lester Pigott ride for you in the Derby is that it gets him off the other fellow's horse.

Vincent O'Brien

When Charlie Cooke sold you a dummy, you had to pay to get back into the ground.

Jim Baxter

There are certain things you don't believe in. The Easter Bunny. Campaign promises. The Abominable Snowman. A husband with lipstick on his collar. And a guy who tells you he shot a 59 on his own ball. Out of town of course.

Jim Murray

 **Sport**

Ally MacLeod thinks that tactics are a new kind of
peppermint.

Billy Connolly

Someone once said that nobody murders Troon. The way I
played the Open there they couldn't even arrest me for
second degree manslaughter.

Lee Trevino

I don't know who designed the Road Hole at St Andrews,
but I hear he's escaped.

Mark James

I don't want to be a millionaire, I only want to live like one.

Walter Hagen

They say, 'Trevino is wondering whether to play a five or a
six iron to the green, when all the time I'm gazing at some
broad in the third row of the gallery, wondering where my
wife is.'

Lee Trevino

My swing is so bad I look like a caveman killing his lunch.

Lee Trevino

I saw Sir Edmund Hillary out there in Saurgrass and he had
to walk around the greens.

Tom Weiskopf

I have a tip that can take five strokes off anyone's golf game. It's called an eraser.

Arnold Palmer

I once played a round with Jack Nicklaus and I asked him what impressed him most about my golf. 'Your score keeping', he replied.

Bob Hope

The biggest mistake I ever made at the Monte Carlo Rally was to let my wife go shopping by herself.

Mario Andretti

Tainton boasted that his mother had given birth to him on the hunting-field after which minor intrusion into a day's sport she went on to be up with the kill at Torne Wood.

John Mortimer

That miss on the red will go straight out of my head as soon as I collect my pension book.

John Parrott

When Peter Beardsley appears on television, daleks hide behind the sofa.

Nick Hancock

You can take a man's wife, you can even take his wallet. But never on any account take a man's putter.

Archie Compston

Sport

Secretariat and Rivia Ridge are the most famous pair of stablemates since Joseph and Mary.

Dick Schaap

I only have to read Joe Louis' name and my nose starts to bleed again.

Tommy Farr

For most amateurs the best wood in the bag is the pencil.

Chi Chi Rodriguez

I was three over: one over a house, one over a patio, and one over a swimming pool.

George Brett

We were so fired up, when the referee ran on to the pitch, three of us tackled him.

Graham Dawe

Gerald Ford made golf a contact sport.

Bob Hope

Snooker is just chess with balls.

Clive James

Arnold Palmer is the biggest crowd pleaser since the invention of the portable sanitary facility.

Bob Hope

When male golfers wiggle their feet to get their stance right they look exactly like cats preparing to pee.

Jilly Cooper

Every team needs a mad bomber with the conscience of a rattlesnake.

Johnny Bach

Putts should be conceded only in the following circumstances:
(i) When your opponent is two inches from the pin and three down.
(ii) Your opponent is nine feet from the hole and is your boss
(iii) Immediately after you have holed out in one.

Tom Scott

Bobby Robson's natural expression is that of a man who fears he may have left the gas on.

David Lacey

The PGA tour has a simple test to see if a player is on drugs – if Isao Aoki speaks and the player understands him, the player is on something.

Bob Hope

I never exaggerate. I just remember big.

Chi Chi Rodriguez

It's not whether you win or lose – but whether I win or lose.

Sandy Lyle

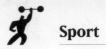

Sport

The ideal board of football directors should be made up of three men – two dead and one dying.

Tommy Docherty

I can close any boxing cut in the world in fifty seconds, so long as it ain't a total beheading.

Adolph Ritacco

It's a marriage. If I had to choose between my wife and my putter – I'd miss her.

Gary Player

The long ball down the middle is like pouring beer down the toilet – it cuts out the middle man.

Jack Charlton

In one year I travelled 450,000 miles by air. That's eighteen and a half times around the world, or once around Howard Cosell's head.

Jackie Stewart

Golf is a game in which the ball lies poorly and the players well.

Art Rosenbaum

I went down to the dugout to pass on some technical information to the team like the fact that the game had started.

Ron Atkinson

Fellows become bookmakers because they are too scared to steal and too heavy to become a jockey.

Noel Whitcome

I've heard it said that sprinters should be allowed to use any drug or other means to improve their performances. Right then I'll have a motor bike.

Paul Merton

In the language of football, 'resign' is a code word meaning 'he was given the choice of quitting, being fired, or having the fans blow up his house'.

Gene Klein

The first ninety minutes of a football match are the most important.

Bobby Robson

Being paired with Arnold Palmer is like a two-shot penalty.

John Schlee

You can hit a 200 acre fairway 10 per cent of the time and a two-inch branch 90 per cent of the time.

Henry Beard

Arnold Palmer has won about as much money playing golf as I've paid on lessons.

Bob Hope

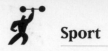

Sport

If Jesus Christ rode his flaming donkey like Jim Old rode that horse, then he deserved to be crucified.

Rod Simpson

Being left-handed is a big advantage. No one knows enough about your swing to mess you up with advice.

Bob Charles

I'm using a new putter because the old one didn't float too well.

Craig Stadler

Sonny Liston is so ugly that when he cries, the tears run down the back of his head.

Mohammed Ali

When I tee the ball where I can see it, I can't hit it. And when I put it where I can hit it, I can't see it.

Jackie Gleason

Songwriter Hoagy Carmichael, an avid golfer, once teed up on a par three hole, picked up a club and hit the ball. It bounced once on the green, hit the pin and dropped in for a hole in one. Hoagy didn't say a word, but took another ball from his pocket, teed up, then observed, 'I think I've got the idea now.'

Buddy Hackett

Arnold Palmer turned golf into a game of 'Hit it hard, go find it and hit it hard again!'

John Schulian

No one who ever had lessons would have a swing like mine.
Lee Trevino

When losing heavily at a game of doubles in tennis, a good ploy is to whisper to one of your opponents when changing ends, 'Your partner is playing very well.'
Michael O'Connell

A caddy is someone who accompanies the golfer and didn't see the ball either.
Joe Francis

Jack Dempsey hits like an epileptic piledriver.
Harry C. Witwert

These are my suggested rules for golf:
Shallow, porcelain-lined open drains sloping in the direction of the green should be introduced at all difficult parts of the course. Every other green should be bowl-shaped with the hole dead in the middle. High rubber walls should be erected around ponds, woods, railway embankments and other hazards. In bunker play any shot which does not propel the ball onto the green or fairway shall not count against the player. Any player who is two or more down may ask his caddie to take every other shot for him. In desperate cases like dormie five, the player may carry the bag and the caddie take all the shots.
John D. Sheridan

He took a swing like a man with a wasp under his shirt and his pants on fire, trying to impale a butterfly on the end of a scythe.

Paul Gallico

The principal difference between Babe Zahanas and myself is that I hit the ball like a girl and she hits the ball like a man.

Bob Hope

If the golfer's object was merely to sink the ball in the hole, he could walk around the course with a bag of golf balls and drop each one in.

Arnold Lunn

The difference between a sand bunker and water is the difference between a car crash and an airplane crash. You have a chance of recovering from a car crash.

Bobby Jones

They asked me if the train passing near the final green hadn't disturbed my putting. I said 'What train?'

Gary Player

Ballesteros spends so much time in the woods that he carries an axe as one of his clubs.

David Feherty

Pessimists see a cup that is half-empty. Optimists see a cup that is half-full. Queens Park Rangers haven't even seen the cup.

Frank Lauder

The most common mistake at St Andrews is just turning up.
Mark James

Driving Mark McCormack's getaway car is the best job in golf.
George Low

The bowling of Cunis, like his name, is neither one thing nor another.
John Arlott

It is hard to tell whether Americans have become such liars because of golf or income tax.
Will Rogers

A real Irish football fan is one who knows the true nationality of every player on the Republic of Ireland team.
Jack Charlton

Arnold Palmer would go for the flag from the middle of an alligator's back.
Lee Trevino

I've never had a coach in my life. When I find one who can beat me, then I'll listen.
Lee Trevino

Never bet with anyone you meet on the first tee who has a deep suntan, a 1 iron in his bag, and squinty eyes.
Dave Marr

The English rugby team – I've seen better centres in a box of Black Magic.

Max Boyce

If it wasn't for golf, I'd be a caddie today.

George Carcher

It hit a spectator, but my ball is OK.

Jerry Pate

To win the US Open, all you have to do is to shoot the lowest score.

Ben Hogan

I cannot understand why people say Ben Hogan is so untalkative. He speaks to me on every green and says, 'You're away.'

Jimmy Demaret

I have finally discovered the secret of the Old Course at St Andrews. Take fewer putts.

Jack Nicklaus

They say I cannot punch, but you should see me putting the cat out at night.

Chris Finnegan

A struggling golfer should take two weeks off and then quit the game.

Jimmy Demaret

What would I have to shoot to win the tournament? The rest of the field.

Roger Maltie

The three ugliest words in golf are – still your shot.

Dave Marr

The reason the pro tells you to keep your head down is so you can't see him laughing.

Phyllis Diller

My car absolutely will not run unless my golf clubs are in the trunk.

Bruce Berlet

A tap-in is a putt that is short enough to be missed one-handed.

Henry Beard

I believe in letting the other guy lose.

Pete Rose

I've hit two balls into the water. I've a good mind to jump in and make it four.

Simon Hobday

Sleep came to Bruce Woodcock, as it must come to all British heavyweights, midway in the fifth round.

Red Smith

My back swing off the first tee put the pro in mind of an elderly woman of dubious morals trying to struggle out of a dress too tight around the shoulders.

Patrick Campbell

I get upset over a bad shot just like anyone else, but it's silly to let the game get to you. When I miss a shot I just think what a beautiful day it is, and what fresh pure air I'm breathing. Then I take a deep breath. I have to do that. That's what gives me the strength to break the club.

Bob Hope

If it wasn't for golf, I don't know what I'd be doing. If my IQ had been two points lower, I'd have been a tree somewhere.

Lee Trevino

Gerald Ford doesn't realise he can't hit a ball through a tree trunk.

Jack Nicklaus

'Stance' is defined by the Rules of Golf as 'that which you have taken up when you place your feet on the ground in position for and preparatory to striking at the ball. The location of the feet before they are placed on the ground is left to the discretion of the individual player.'

John D. Sheridan

We've lost seven of our last eight matches. The only team that we have beaten is Western Samoa. It's a good job we didn't play the whole of Samoa.

Gareth Davies

Don't talk about Michael Johnson's style. Look, if that guy ran with his fingers up his bum he could still run 42 seconds for 400 metres.

Roger Black

There is only one man allowed to say 'There's nothing wrong with defeat', and that's Nelson Mandela's chiropodist.

Jack Powell

Saint Paul was the first golfer – he fought the good fight and finished the course.

Billy Graham

Always remember your bones cannot break in a bobsleigh – they shatter.

John Candy

Paul Ince with a big white bandage on his head was running around the field looking like a pint of Guinness.

Paul Gascoigne

Bob Hope has a beautiful short game. Unfortunately it's off the tee.

Jimmy Demaret

Colin Montgomerie is a few fries short of a happy meal. His mind goes on vacation and leaves his mouth in charge.

David Feherty

Jack Lemmon has been in more bunkers than Eva Braun.
Phil Harris

We lost the test through fifteen-man rugby. It was just that we didn't have the ball.
Ian McGeechan

I had a rather bizarre telephone call with Kenny Dalglish and I understood only part of it. I assume it was a bad line.
Victor Green

Few pleasures on earth match the feeling that comes from making a loud bodily function noise just as the other guy is about to putt.
Dave Barry

One of the O'Flanagan twins who played rugby for Ireland was punched by a French forward but the other twin persuaded the referee not to send him off. However, the twins did ensure that the French forward eventually left the field – on a stretcher.
Richard Harris

My only feeling about superstition is that it's unlucky to be behind at the end of the game.
Duffy Dougherty

No matter how I try I just can't seem to break 64.
Jack Nicklaus

The best thing you can do with a horse that hangs left is to put a bit of lead in his right ear to act as a counterbalance – with a shotgun.

Lester Piggott

Manchester City are the only team in the world to get the crowd to autograph the ball after the game.

Bernard Manning

Hubert Green swings like a drunk trying to find a keyhole in the dark.

Jim Murray

If you can keep your head when all about you are losing theirs, you're at the wrong end of the football pitch.

Bill Munro

Basketball is a simple game to understand. Players race up and down a fairly small area indoors and stuff the ball into a ring with Madonna's dress hanging on it.

Dan Jenkins

Any money I put on a horse is a sort of insurance policy to prevent it from winning.

Frank Richardson

England's coach Jack Rowell, an immensely successful businessman, has the acerbic wit of Dorothy Parker and, according to most New Zealanders, a similar knowledge of rugby.

Mark Reason

I sometimes got birthday cards from fans. But it's always the same message – they hope it's my last.

Al Norman

What do I think of William Shakespeare? I'll moider da bum!

Tony Galento

Seve Ballesteros drives into territory Daniel Boone couldn't find.

Fuzzy Zoeller

The key to an ice hockey match is the first punch. If you're left-handed and they're expecting a right, it helps a lot.

Wayne Cashman

It's easy to beat Brazil. You just stop them getting twenty yards from your goal.

Bobby Charlton

A puck is a hard rubber disc that ice hockey players strike when they can't hit each other.

Jimmy Cannon

In football it is widely accepted that if both sides agree to cheat then cheating is fair.

Charles B. Fry

It ain't getting it that hurts my players, it's staying up all night looking for it. They got to learn that if you don't get it by midnight, you ain't gonna get it, and if you do, it ain't worth it.

Casey Stengel

Mountain climbers rope themselves together to prevent the sensible ones from going home.

Earl Wilson

Ice hockey is a form of disorderly conduct in which a score is kept.

Doug Larson

I watched the Indy 500, and I was thinking that if they left earlier they wouldn't have to go so fast.

Steven Wright

We are in such a slump that even the ones that aren't drinkin' aren't hittin'.

Casey Stengel

The only time I feel superstitious is when somebody hits me hard on the chin.

Jack Dempsey

Sport

The sole Dutch Guiana entrant in the 1956 Olympics was runner Wim Esajas. He slept all morning to relax for the event and arrived at the stadium at 2 p.m. only to learn that the race had been run in the morning. He returned home where he was beheaded.

Peter Sherwood

I would not advise any golf professional to marry until after the age of thirty. Marriage demands a division of interests and golf, particularly tournament golf, demands every minute of a man's attention.

Henry Cotton

The present state of English rugby is serious but not hopeless; the present state of Irish rugby is hopeless but not serious.

Noel Henderson

Theatre and Criticism

Don't pay any attention to the critics. Don't even ignore them.

Sam Goldwyn

The unique thing about Margaret Rutherford is that she can act with her chin alone.

Kenneth Tynan

The crowd were behind me all the way, but I shook them off at the railway station.

Tom O'Connor

My dear delightful company, I have just watched your performance of *The Importance of Being Earnest*. It reminds me of a play I once wrote.

Oscar Wilde

The trouble with nude dancing is that not everything stops when the music stops.

Robert Helpmann

A politically correct American revival of *Guys and Dolls* is to be called *Loathsome Oppressors and Women of Vision and Strength*!

Nigel Rees

Danny La Rue denies that he is a wealthy man, but I happen to know for a fact that he has a little bit tucked away.

Jimmy Tarbuck

I want my Hamlet to be so male that when I come out on the stage, they can hear my balls clank.

John Barrymore

W.H. Auden's face looks like a wedding cake left out in the rain.

Stephen Spender

The trouble with Freud is that he never had to play the old Glasgow Empire on a Saturday night after Rangers and Celtic had both lost.

Ken Dodd

We would see Charles Laughton floating in his own pool and it was just the reverse of an iceberg – 90 per cent of him was visible.

Peter Ustinov

This must be an extremely wealthy town – I see that each of you bought two or three seats.

Victor Borge

Edith Evans took her curtain calls as though she had just been un-nailed from the cross.

Noel Coward

Eddie Izzard is a comedian so politically correct that he wears a skirt.

Paul Vallely

To people who say to me that the Abbey Theatre is not what it used to be, I reply 'It never was'.

Lennox Robinson

Kylie Minogue looks like one of those nine-year-olds from Dagenham done up in her mother's lipstick, to appear on a talent show.

Jonathan Margolis

If you were a shape-changing movie creature, needing a supply of virgins to survive, would you choose to live in America?

Simon Rose

Dear Ingrid Bergman – speaks five languages and can't act in any of them.

John Gielgud

I can't say it was the worst ever *Richard II*, because I imagine that in Upper Volta there may have been school productions for English-as-a-second-language classes, but, it must have been a close-run thing.

A.A. Gill

Trying to direct Robert Morley was about as useful as trying to alter the sequence on a set of traffic lights.

John Gielgud

I've always thought I would be particularly good in Romeo and Juliet – as the nurse.

Noel Coward

The script of *Murder One* is as tight as an egg-fed nun's bum.

A.A. Gill

I once stayed in a theatrical boarding house that had two toilets, one upstairs and one downstairs. There was one rule that you broke at your peril – no solids downstairs.

Les Dawson

Very few people go to the doctor when they have a cold. They go to the theatre instead.

W. Boyd Gatewood

In the ballet suddenly Sigmund hears the flutter of wings, and a group of wild swans flies across the moon. Sigmund is astounded to see that their leader is part-swan and part-woman – unfortunately, divided lengthwise. She enchants Sigmund, who is careful not to make any poultry jokes.

Woody Allen

Even Donald Sinden managed to put aside his habitual act of Queen Victoria playing Widow Twankey to turn in a heavyweight country-class lord.

A.A. Gill

Milton Berle knows the secret of making people laugh and he sure knows how to keep a secret.

Arnold Strang

At my most recent performance the audience were so tightly packed they could not applaud horizontally; they had to applaud vertically.

W.C. Fields

A drama critic has the same effect on one as a bicycle without a saddle.

Brendan Behan

Very good actors never talk about their art. Very bad ones never stop.

John Whiting

With the collapse of vaudeville new talent has no place to stink.

George Burns

My favourite comedian is Frank Carson. Over the years I have enjoyed his joke very much.

Ken Dodd

Critics – the very word suggests an insect.

Dylan Moran

I once had a nightmare in which I heard the judge say, 'The prisoner is sentenced to face a mixed audience of St Louisians, Washingtonians and Kansas Citizens every night for the remainder of his life. Bailiff, lead him to the theatre and let the punishment begin'.

W.C. Fields

The question actors most often get asked is how they can bear saying the same things over and over again night after night, but God knows the answer to that is, don't we all anyway; might as well get paid for it.

Elaine Dundy

If there is one pleasure on earth which surpasses all others, it is leaving a play before the end. I might perhaps except the joy of taking tickets for a play, dining well, sitting on after dinner, and finally not going at all. That of course, is very heaven.

Angela Thirkell

Shaw has the emotional range of a Pat Boone record with a scratch.

A. A. Gill

To me Edith Evans looks like something that would eat its young.

Dorothy Parker

I am a Camera – Me no Leica.

Walter Kerr

I spent four years studying mime under Marcel Marceau – unfortunately he was teaching welding at the time.

Paul Merton

I won't play Hamlet unless he gives me a stroke a hole.

Groucho Marx

Jackie Collins is to writing what her sister Joan is to acting.
Campbell Grison

The first thing a comedian does on getting an unscheduled laugh is to verify the state of his buttons.
Alva Johnston

Better an eternity in Hell with Little and Large, Max Bygraves and Dick Emery than a single Christmas with the Osmonds.
Clive James

Dustin Hoffman is the luckiest Jewish midget that ever lived.
Martin Rackin

Samantha Fox in a leather suit looks like a badly wrapped black pudding.
Janet Street-Porter

Mrs Siddons was so dramatic she stabbed the potatoes at dinner.
Sydney Smith

The consistent thing about all American courtroom drama is that invariably the only vaguely human being on the credits is the psycho multiple murderer.
A.A. Gill

It was without doubt the most cringe-making, knuckle-chewing livivacious bit of screamingly ghastly dramatic television ever – and I haven't forgotten Brian Blessed going up Everest.

A.A. Gill

Groucho Marx was a major comedian, which is to say that he had the compassion of an icicle, the effrontery of a carnival shill and the generosity of a pawnbroker.

S.J. Perelman

The first time I saw Barbra Streisand perform she was so good, I wanted to run up to the stage, put my arms around her – and wring her neck.

Judy Garland

The best heckle I ever had was one night when I went on stage and said I was going to do the weatherman sketch. 'Here is the weather,' I began – Meteorologist,' shouted a bloke from the audience.

Malcolm Hardee

All my shows are great. Some of them are bad. But they're all great.

Lew Grade

Some critics are emotionally desiccated, personally about as attractive as a year-old peach in a single girl's refrigerator.

Mel Brooks

Heywood Broun once described Geoffrey Steyne as the worst actor on the American stage. Steyne sued but lost the case. The next time Broun reviewed a play in which Steyne appeared he said simply 'Mr Steyne's performance was not up to its usual standard.'

Robert E. Drennan

Avoid crowds during the influenza epidemic – see *Someone in the House*.

George S. Kaufman

In a 1956 production of *King Lear* in New York, Orson Welles, who had fractured his ankle in a fall, played the title role from a wheelchair.

Mark Fowler

I have more talent in my smallest fart than Barbra Streisand has in her entire body.

Walter Matthau

Bo Derek turned down the role of Helen Keller because she couldn't remember the lines.

Joan Rivers

Critics – unless the bastards have the courage to give you unqualified praise, I say ignore them.

John Steinbeck

After my act there was a lot of booing but also a lot of clapping. But the clapping was for the booing.

Milton Berle

Miscellaneous

Miscellaneous

We don't necessarily discriminate. We simply exclude certain types of people.

Gerald Wellman

Show me a man who is content, and I'll show you a lobotomy scar.

Sean Connery

It happened as quick as a flashlight.

Sam Goldwyn

How come the dove gets to be the peace symbol? How about the pillow? It has more feathers than the dove, and it doesn't have that dangerous beak.

Jack Handey

'Aviatrix' means deceased person.

Dave Barry

Rolf Harris is the only performer that dogs can ask for by name – Rolf, Rolf.

A.A. Gill

There are many strange jobs on offer in the country. I once met a chap whose job it was to stick the chicken crap and feathers onto free range eggs so you knew they were the real thing.

Craig Charles

'You haven't got the guts to pull that trigger' is almost always a bad thing to say.

Russell Bell

This *Travel Guide* is dedicated to Wilbur and Orville Wright without whom airsickness would still be just a dream.

Dave Barry

Ariana Stassinopoulos is so boring that you fall asleep halfway through her name.

Alan Bennett

When in doubt, go shopping.

Sarah Ferguson

Marshal Foch was just a frantic pair of moustaches.

T.E. Lawrence

His neck was the width of a fat man's thigh. He looked like Lou Feringo's idiot cousin.

Zoë Heller

Not enough farmers give their sheep pocket money.

Charlie Chuck

When I was told that curiosity killed the cat, I asked what exactly the cat was so curious about.

Wright Stevens

A liberal is a man who is too broadminded to take his own side in an argument.

Robert Frost

We do try to anticipate your questions so that I can respond 'no comment' with some degree of knowledge.

William Baker

I propose getting rid of conventional armaments and replacing them with reasonably priced hydrogen bombs that would be distributed equally throughout the world.

Idi Amin

When Fortune empties her chamberpot on your head, smile and say, 'We are going to have a summer shower'.

John A. MacDonald

Generals detest generals on their own side far more than they dislike the enemy.

Peter Ustinov

Look wise, say nothing, and grunt. Speech was given to conceal thought.

William Osler

How many whales do we really need? I figure five. One for each ocean. We save their semen in a huge mayonnaise jar, we procreate them when we need to.

Denis Leary

Miscellaneous

This is Bollocks the butler speaking. What splendid news about mad-cow disease. That explains the last twenty years and I thought I was the one who was barmy. Please leave a spring-like message after the Moooooooo.

Willie Rushton

How do the men who drive the snow plough get to work in the morning?

Steven Wright

There are four things that will never come back: the spoken word; the speeding arrow; the past and hot pants.

Russell Bell

F.E. Smith is very clever, but sometimes his brains go to his head.

Margot Asquith

I have often wished to cultivate modesty, but I am too busy thinking about myself.

Edith Sitwell

Tragedy is when I cut my finger. Comedy is when you fall into an open sewer and die.

Mel Brooks

Like most of those who study history, Napoleon III learned from the mistakes of the past how to make new ones.

A.J.P. Taylor

Miscellaneous

Let the scintillations of your wit be like the coruscations of summer lightning, lambent but innocuous.

Edward Goulbum

I don't believe in fairies, even if they exist.

Brendan Behan

Turbulence is what pilots announce that you have encountered when your plane strikes an object in midair.

Dave Barry

Brevity is the.

Kevin Gildea

It rolled off my back like a duck.

Sam Goldwyn

It's like carrying something or other, somewhere or other, as the case may be.

W.C. Fields

I played a lot of tough clubs in my time. Once a guy in one of those clubs wanted to bet me $10 that I was dead. I was afraid to bet.

Henny Youngman

Monogamy is OK in the office but at home I prefer white pine.

Samuel Goldwyn

Woke up this morning, I was folding my bed back into a couch. I almost broke both my arms because it's not one of those kind of beds.

Steven Wright

I once heard two ladies going on and on about the pains of childbirth and how men don't seem to know what real pain is. I asked them if either of them ever got themselves caught in a zipper.

Emo Philips

The other day on the underground I stood up and enjoyed the pleasure of offering my seat to three ladies.

G.K. Chesterton

I wonder what language truck drivers are using now that everyone else is using theirs.

Beryl Pfizer

Generals are fascinating cases of arrested development – after all, at five we all of us wanted to be generals.

Peter Ustinov

It is nice to make heroic decisions and to be prevented by 'circumstances beyond your control' from ever trying to execute them.

William James

And it is written, a wise man never plays leapfrog with a unicorn.

Emo Philips

Miscellaneous

The Army is a place where you get up early in the morning to be yelled at by people with short haircuts and tiny brains.

Dave Barry

How do pebbles know how to get into a shoe, but never know how to get out?

Casper Dante

I've just signed a contract to do commercials for a mattress company and fulfilled my life's ambition. I'll get paid for lying down.

Lee Trevino

[Anything in parenthesis can be ignored].

Bill Seeger

I may not agree with what you say but if you say it I'll punch you in the mouth.

Laurence J. Peter

If the phone doesn't ring, it's me.

Jimmy Durante

How would I like to be remembered? In somebody's will.

Robert Redford

Everywhere is within walking distance if you have the time.

Steven Wright

In any organisation there will always be one person who knows what is going on. That man must be fired.

John Conway

I cannot stand this proliferation of paperwork. It's useless to fight the forms. You've got to kill the people producing them.

Vladimir Kabaidze

Predicting the future is easy. It's trying to figure out what's going on now that's hard.

Fritz Dressler

Why do kamikaze pilots wear helmets? Smacks of indecision to me.

Sean Meo

You've no idea what a poor opinion I have of myself – and how little I deserve it.

W.S. Gilbert

Nero renamed the month of April after himself, calling it Neroreus, but the idea never caught on because April is not Neroreus and there is no use pretending that it is.

Will Cuppy

If Dracula cannot see his reflection in the mirror, how come his hair is always so neatly combed?

Steven Wright

Whenever I pick up someone hitchhiking I always like to wait for a few minutes before I say anything to them. Then I say, 'Put your seatbelt on – I wanna try something. I saw it in a cartoon but I'm pretty sure I can do it.'

Steven Wright

I may have faults but being wrong ain't one of them.

Jimmy Hoffa

Those press-on towels are a real rip-off aren't they? I used six of them and I couldn't even get my arms dry.

Jack Dee

If Dorothy Parker isn't more careful with her suicide attempts, one of these days she's going to hurt herself.

Alexander Woolcott

The private papers left by Herbert Morrison were so dull and banal that they would have to be burned to provide any illumination at all.

John Zametica

Once at the airport I leaped onto the conveyor belt just as the luggage was coming through. When the airport police arrived I said to them, 'Just one more round and I promise to get off. I've always wanted to do this, all my life.'

Spike Milligan

The main thing about being a hero is to know when to die. Prolonged life has ruined a great number of heroes.

Will Rogers

Mutiny is such an unpleasant word – think of it more as a management reshuffle.

Alistair Swinerton

Cheops built the Great Pyramid of Gizeh about 3050 BC. Then he felt better.

Will Cuppy

There is nothing so pathetic as a forgetful liar.

F.M. Knowles

Third class mail – what's that? They strap the letter to a crazy person and he wanders at random.

Richard Lewis

I'm so unlucky that if I was to fall into a barrel of nipples I'd come out sucking my thumb.

Freddie Starr

Work is the refuge of people who have nothing better to do.

Oscar Wilde

I got a new dog. He's a paranoid retriever. He brings back everything because he's not sure what I threw him.

Steven Wright

But enough of me, let's talk about you. What do you think of me?

Ed Koch

There are two classes of pedestrian – the quick and the dead.

George Robey

How long was I in the army? Five foot eleven.

Spike Milligan

He flung himself upon his horse and rode madly off in all directions.

Stephen Leacock

A coward dies a hundred deaths, a brave man only once. But then once is enough isn't it?

Harry Stone

Nothing I do can't be done by a ten-year-old with twenty-five years of practice.

Harry Blackstone

I've just solved the parking problem. I bought a parked car.

Henny Youngman

One can survive everything nowadays, except death.

Oscar Wilde

My idea of exercise is a good brisk sit.

Phyllis Diller

A Jiffy Bag is an envelope used to alert Post Office employees to damage opportunities.

Mike Barfield

If only I had a little humility, I'd be perfect.

Ted Turner

The general idea in any first class laundry is to see that no shirt or collar ever comes back twice.

Stephen Leacock

He was a self-made man who owed his lack of success to nobody.

Joseph Heller

I regard you with an indifference closely bordering on aversion.

Robert Louis Stevenson

A lady came up to me on the street and pointed to my suede jacket. 'You know a cow was murdered for that jacket?' she sneered. I replied in a psychotic tone, 'I didn't know there were any witnesses. Now I'll have to kill you too.'

Jake Johanson

If there are two or more ways to do something, and one of those ways can result in a catastrophe, then someone will do it.

Edward Murphy

Yesterday I told a chicken to cross the road. It said 'Why?'

Steven Wright

Miscellaneous

In theory there is no difference between theory and practice, but in practice there is.

J.L. Van De Snapscheut

Index

Index

Index

Index

Index

Index

Index

Index

Index

Index

Index